CONCILIUM

CONCILIUM
ADVISORY COMMITTEE

GREGORY BAUM	*Montreal, QC* Canada
JOSÉ OSCAR BEOZZO	*São Paulo, SP* Brazil
WIM BEUKEN	*Louvain* Belgium
LEONARDO BOFF	*Petrópolis, RJ* Brazil
JOHN COLEMAN	*Los Angeles, CA* USA
CHRISTIAN DUQUOC	*Lyon* France
VIRGIL ELIZONDO	*San Antonio, TX* USA
SEAN FREYNE	*Dublin* Ireland
CLAUDE GEFFRÉ	*Paris* France
NORBERT GREINACHER	*Tübingen* Germany
GUSTAVO GUTIÉRREZ	*Lima* Peru
HERMANN HÄRING	*Tübingen* Germany
WERNER G. JEANROND	*Glasgow* Scotland
JEAN-PIERRE JOSSUA	*Paris* France
MAUREEN JUNKER-KENNY	*Dublin* Ireland
FRANÇOIS KABASELE LUMBALA	*Kinshasa* Dem. Rep. of Congo
NICHOLAS LASH	*Cambridge* England
MARY-JOHN MANANZAN	*Manila* Philippines
ALBERTO MELLONI	*Reggio Emilia* Italy
NORBERT METTE	*Münster* Germany
DIETMAR MIETH	*Tübingen* Germany
JÜRGEN MOLTMANN	*Tübingen* Germany
TERESA OKURE	*Port Harcourt* Nigeria
ALOYSIUS PIERIS	*Kelaniya, Colombo* Sri Lanka
DAVID POWER	*Washington, D.C.* USA
GIUSEPPE RUGGIERI	*Catania* Italy
PAUL SCHOTSMANS	*Louvain* Belgium
JANET MARTIN SOSKICE	*Cambridge* England
ELSA TAMEZ	*San José* Costa Rica
CHRISTOPH THEOBALD	*Paris* France
DAVID TRACY	*Chicago, IL* USA
MARCIANO VIDAL	*Madrid* Spain
ELLEN VAN WOLDE	*Tilburg* Holland

CONCILIUM 2012/5

WATER MARKS OUR LIFE

Edited by

Solange Lefebvre and Marie-Theres Wacker

SCM Press · London

Published in 2012 by SCM Press, 3rd Floor, Invicta House, 108–114 Golden Lane, London EC1Y 0TG.

SCM Press is an imprint of Hymns Ancient & Modern Ltd (a registered charity) 13A Hellesdon Park Road, Norwich NR6 5DR, UK

Copyright © International Association of Conciliar Theology, Madras (India)

www.concilium.in

English translations copyright © 2012 Hymns Ancient & Modern Ltd.

All rights reserved. No part of this publication may be reproduced, stored in a retrieval system, or transmitted, in any form or by any means, electronic, mechanical, photocopying or otherwise, without the prior written permission of the Board of Directors of Concilium.

ISBN 9780334031215

Printed in the UK by
CPI Antony Rowe, Chippenham, Wiltshire

Concilium is published in March, June, August, October, December

Contents

Editorial
Water Marks Our Life 7

Part One: Contexts

Water in Danger 13
LENA PARTZSCH

'My God, it's our river, shouldn't we preserve it? Without the river, what else have we got? 24
SYLVIE SHAW

Water in the Old Testament 36
ERHARD S. GERSTENBERGER

Water as Sacrament: Global Water Crisis and Sacramental Stewardship 46
MARK L. ALLMAN

'Give me this water. . .': The Water of Life in John's Gospel 58
PIERRE LETOURNEAU

African Women and Water 68
ANNE-BEATRICE FAYE CIC

Feminine Waterscapes: Water as a Gendered Subject 78
KUNTALA LAHIRI-DUTT

Life, Water and Liberation 88
MARCELO BARROS

Part Two: Experiences

Reading the Bible after Fukushima   99
KUMIKO KATO

A Bridge that Divides: The Bridge of Mostar   105
ŽELJKO IVANKOVIĆ

WATER in Action   112
MARY E. HUNT

Making Peace with Water   117
LUIS INFANTI DE LA MORA OSM

Part Three: Forum

Kateri Tekekwitha: the First Indigenous Saint of North America   123
BERNADETTE RIGAL-CELLAR

Women as Pioneers at Vatican II   129
IDA RAMING

Contributors   137

Editorial
Water Marks Our Life

This issue of *Concilium* is devoted to water, an extremely rich and deep topic for theology and for pastoral work. As editors, we were impressed by the strength of the contributions which the theme elicited. In the eighteenth century, the German theologian Johann Albert Fabricius (1668–1736) published *Hydrotheologie* (Hydrotheology), a theology of water, and a systematic treatise on God's goodness, wisdom and power as manifested in its creation. More recently, almost all branches of theology, such as biblical studies, systematic theology, spirituality, ethics, feminist theology and pastoral theology, have addressed the theme.

Water has become immensely important in our own times. It is still in short supply in many parts of the world where people are constantly thirsty, and it is still the cause of, or excuse for, cruel wars. Even when water is abundant, it can turn into a devastating threat in the form of tsunamis and hurricanes. The biblical flood can suddenly become horribly relevant nowadays. Water is also a resource with major territorial associations, and there are disputes about its control in many parts of the world, including the Arctic, where the ice is melting and the sea level is rising. For some scientists, the former or current presence of water is a sign of life on other planets.

Whether life-giving or annihilating, water is a major biblical symbol and an essential part of the imagery of our tradition, from the Spirit hovering over the waters, the flood narrative, and the soul thirsting for God in the Psalms, through the baptism of Jesus, his use of water in his public life, to his death and the symbolic release of blood and water from his body. Over the centuries, water has been a central topic in Christian sacraments, rites and creative works. More recently, it has become an important theme in, say, gender studies, with symbolic reference to

Editorial

women's lives, especially motherhood, and practical relevance to women's exhausting labour as water-carriers in so many countries.

This issue of *Concilium* brings together authoritative contributions on this highly-nuanced subject, prompting serious reflections on the theological, symbolical, spiritual, political, ethical and pastoral significance of water.

Lena Partzsch writes as a political scholar on water in danger. She gives an overall account of the many problems the planet is facing in this respect: water shortage, water conflicts and water wars. She indicates the growing importance of global governance, international agreements on water politics, interrelated aspects of politics and economics, inter-state regulations, trans-national trusts and NGOs. She describes the possible remedies offered by social entrepreneurs developing new solutions for ecological and social problems. Sylvie Shaw, an expert in religious studies from Australia, where water is accessible but threatened by urban pollution, presents the results of illuminating research into the links between the population of a town and the Brisbane River running through it. She reminds us of the history of water buried in the memories of witnesses of urbanization, often at the expense of water and the lives associated with it. A study of local residents' experiences of the river reveals the often profound aspects of their relationship with it.

Three articles are concerned with biblical and sacramental theology. Erhard Gerstenberger, a biblical scholar, provides a widely-referenced account of water in the Old Testament. He reminds us that the Hebrew Bible does not contain any systematic 'water doctrine' but a highly varied tapestry of experiences, and traditional themes and motifs, often originating in Mesopotamia. He categorizes these images and metaphors under three headings: the destructive force and chaos of 'evil water'; the human experience of rainwater and wells, and reliance on them; and 'spiritualizations', from the dualism of the well-watered paradise and the underworld with its non-existent or non-potable water to such theological metaphors as the similarity between the importance of God and that of water (Ps. 42.2–3). Pierre Létourneau, a Canadian exegete, discusses the narrative sequence of Jesus' meeting with the Samaritan woman at the well (John 4.1–42) to illustrate the exchange or bestowal of water representing the human experience of God. The complex use of water in John's gospel is shown to range from Jesus' revelatory word begetting eternal life in the believer to the Spirit of truth pouring from his body on the cross. From a sacramental and ethical viewpoint, Mark Allman, an American theologian, examines the extent of the global water crisis (including access, sanitation and privatization, and the role of human ingenuity and labour in making water potable and available). He discusses the function of creation in sacramental life (especially that of water in baptism) with emphasis on the maxim *lex orandi, lex credendi, lex vivendi, lex agendi*. He proposes a theology of water as sacrament and reminds us of the Christian obligation to address the global water crisis as a duty of justice and sacramental stewardship.

Three contributions offer practical and symbolic reflections on water in Africa, South America and India. Beatrice Fayé, an African thinker, and Kuntala Lahiri-Dutt, an Indian commentator working in religious studies, describe the complex relations between gender and water. Fayé reminds us that numerous Africans and people without water throughout the world know the real meaning of thirst and therefore of the Samaritan-woman narrative in the New Testament. Very many African women work long and hard hours to obtain water for their families, expose themselves to violence, and deprive themselves of study and recreation. The symbolic and spiritual significance of water is interwoven with countless aspects of everyday life. Fayé echoes the social and papal teaching of the Church on the need for free access to water. Lahiri-Dutt explores Hinduism to show how water has been viewed as a gendered physical element in India, and concentrates not only on traditional Sanskrit texts that describe water holistically as part of nature, but on Indian folk images of rivers. She tries to re-conceptualize water with a stronger emphasis on ecology and spirituality rather than on current instrumental and functionalist approaches, and with attention to the interplay between power and 'water-decisions'.

Marcelo Barros, a Brazilian theologian, offers a critical view of capitalism, which he sees as reducing water to the level of a mere resource, whereas water is a universal human concern calling for the concentrated attention of theology and Christian spirituality. He provides an overview of the meaning of water in the Bible and other religious traditions, and the numerous fora and texts produced by the United Nations on the problem of poverty and water, as well as a summary account of what might be an appropriate pastoral approach to water in the present-day world.

Four short articles connect variously with the central theme of this

Editorial

issue. Kumiko Kato, a Japanese biblical scholar, writes about the direct relevance of the Bible after the Fukushima disaster, and raises the questions of guilt and responsibility. The Croatian writer Željko Ivanković tells the moving story of the Bridge of Mostar, an architectural masterpiece and cultural treasure that was destroyed and recently rebuilt. The Chilean Bishop Luis Infanti calls for strong pastoral leadership on the distribution of water resources, and Mary Hunt, an American theologian, describes WATER, a highly original Christian network.

Our Forum this month features two articles. Bernadette Rigal Cellar, a French sociologist, offers a basic introduction to the recently-canonized Kateri Tekakwitha, the first indigenous saint of North America. Ida Raming, a German theologian, recalls the pioneer efforts of women at Vatican II and asks for a reconsideration of the Church's teaching on women and their exclusion from the priesthood.

We are especially grateful for the advice and help of Diego Irrazaval, Susan Ross, Felix Wilfred, Eamonn Conway, Rosino Gibellini, Sylvie Shaw, Marco Moerschbacher and Marcel König.

Solange Lefebvre, Marie-Theres Wacker

Part One: Contexts

Water in Danger

LENA PARTZSCH

I Introduction

'Rio+20', the 'Earth Summit', or United Nations Conference on Sustainable Development, was held in Rio de Janeiro, Brazil, on 20–22 June 2012. Even now, 20 years after the first Earth Summit, the persistent demand for natural resources such as water is a vast challenge. Admittedly 75 per cent of planet earth is covered in water, but most of this is salt water, a brackish liquid, or ice and snow. Less than 4 per cent of the water on the earth's surface is available as liquid fresh water, a resource seriously threatened by excessive use and pollution.[1] A fundamental transformation is needed to protect our water sources and to ensure that they are in an ecologically favourable state.[2] Almost one billion people worldwide have no access to clean drinking water and more than double that number lack any sanitary facilities.[3]

I shall devote the first part of this article to the main challenges in this respect, the scarcity of freshwater resources and the resulting conflicts, which I shall examine from the viewpoint of the social and political sciences. In the second part I shall discuss the aims of international attempts to resolve these problems, and ways of implementing them. The overall question is what we should do to make sure that water is used equably and sustainably.

II Growing scarcity of fresh water

Only 10 per cent of worldwide water consumption takes place directly in private households. The highest water use (at over 70 per cent) is that of agricultural food production, followed by industry at about 20 per cent.[4] For instance, 1000 litres of water are needed to produce one litre of milk: for growing fodder plants, for the cow itself, for the farm operation, and for further processing of the milk. More than 1300 litres of water are needed to produce one kilogram of bread.[5] The term 'virtual water' has been devised to describe water needed to obtain a product yet no longer visible in the end-product. Another 5158 litres of virtual water are added to the approximately 130 litres of water per capita used directly in e.g. German households as drinking water, for cooking or for other domestic requirements.[6]

Water use is excessive especially where there is a high proportion of irrigation agriculture, e.g. the Indio-Ganges plateau in Southern Asia, the Northern Chinese plateau and the high-plateau regions of North America.[7] Conventional industrialized agriculture also uses chemical fertilizers (phosphates, nitrates and pesticides), which have a deleterious effect on water, for instance by inducing algae proliferation. Nitrates from large-scale stock raising are now a major problem for water quality in many Western European countries. The costs of treatment are borne by the individual water users and not by the farmers responsible for the pollution. Moreover, the sustained assault on water supplies now means that it is no longer possible to restore the original water quality.

The globalization of trade means that products such as foodstuffs are less often consumed where they are produced. This leads to the ludicrous situation of Europe importing virtual water from drought-ridden Africa and helping to hasten the excessive use and pollution of resources there,[8] although European consumers are unaware of their responsibility in this regard. The virtual water used in Germany, for example, is 58.7 per cent imported.[9] Domestic water resources are protected at the expense of producer countries, especially by importing agricultural products. The water-intensive production of flowers for export, for instance, has almost exhausted Lake Naivasha in Kenya. This lake is used by more than 350 species of birds, hippopotamuses, buffalos, apes and other diminishing animal populations, and by nomadic Masai herdsmen who rely on it to water their cattle. 'In this way, the flower enthusiasts of distant countries unknowingly whittle away at the basis of existence of that part of the population with no share in the profits of flower growing.'[10]

The shortage of water is increasing mainly because of an intensified demand resulting from population growth, persistent urbanization and economic development, together with new patterns of consumption (e.g., more meat consumption). The vagaries of climate change contribute to this process.[11] Water precipitation is an essential element of climate. The changes in climate provoked by increased carbon dioxide and other greenhouse gases will lead to a fundamental transformation of the global water cycle. Water availability will be considerably reduced in certain countries and areas such as Northern China, whereas the volume of water will increase in others, as in Bangladesh. Even in Europe, we are already observing an increase in extreme weather phenomena, such as torrential rains, floods and drought.[12]

Climate change also threatens to disturb water storage, a 'service' performed by the natural hydrologic cycle that is essential to life for hundreds of big cities and millions of hectares of irrigated land.[13] Glaciers and snow-fields in the mountains operate as gigantic natural water reservoirs. They feed the world's big rivers. For some decades now glaciers have been melting in many mountainous regions such as the Alps.[14] For a limited time the melting of the glaciers will increase the flow rate and provide regional suppliers with a temporary rise in the water supply. But if the glaciers disappear, the water reserves and outlets which they supply will also decline and dry up in the medium term.

The global per capita water availability is constantly diminishing.[15] Until 2000 thirty countries were affected by an absolute water shortage with an annual natural water availability of less than 500 m^3 per capita. Eight more countries could be added to this list by 2025. Furthermore, 16 countries suffer from a relative water scarcity with less than 1000 m^3 of annual per capita water availability. The Near East with its conflicts about the water from the Euphrates, Tigris and Jordan is cited in support of the thesis that this water shortage provokes cross-border conflicts.[16] Yet it is precisely in the environmental field that we observe greater cooperation between States with regard to resources such as water. By now international collaboration has ensured the provision of more than 200 environmental treaties and conventions and a whole range of institutional structures for their supervision, implementation and reinforcement.[17]

III Water conflicts

The change in the perception of water to that of an increasingly scarce asset has provoked new conflicts. The scarcer clean water becomes, the more valuable it is. Accordingly, many commentators argue that the 'true' price of water should be controlled by market mechanisms. They say that the fact that water costs little or nothing and the finding that the infrastructure for water use is generally publicly financed, are the main reasons for the ever-greater shortage of resources.[18] The systematic application of fees and charges should (they say) drastically reduce water wastage and pollution. Furthermore, the extension and operation of water supplies in developmental cooperation should be (re-)financed by means of water prices in order to reduce the burden on public budgets.[19] Private companies have become involved in the water business over the last two decades, in half of all countries, and especially in industrial but also in developing nations.

Water as a business continues to arouse strong protests. The opposing sides in this conflict are those interests advocating water prices and privatization of supplies, and those who indeed support water pricing to some extent (cost coverage and the break-even principle), but believe in continued public supplies and universal access. Non-governmental organizations (NGOs) are the main opponents of the privatization of supply structures, and particularly of transnational companies taking over supplies, since then private profit would be the main motivation. Water prices are always problematical if people cannot afford them. Market mechanisms cut off water supplies for anyone who can't pay.

Conflicts have also taken on violent aspects. In the last decade and a half the 'water wars' in Cochabamba, Bolivia, have been the most prominent signs of this tendency. More than 100 people have been injured and several others killed during protests against Bechtel, a private water company.[20] Numerous civil campaigns have insisted that water is a human right and not a market commodity. No one should be deprived of water only because he or she cannot pay the price demanded for the 'primary human nutrient'.[21]

IV International water objectives

In July 2010, after more than a decade of intensive socially-committed campaigning, the right to clean water was adopted in the Universal Declaration of Human Rights.[22] This resolution did not make the right to clean water legally enforceable, but was a clear indication of the urgency of sustainable water provision. Water had acquired a new priority on the global agenda.

On an international level, it was the International Conference on Water and the Environment (ICWE) held in Dublin in 1992 which offered a sophisticated presentation of fresh water as a limited resource and economic asset. The principles put forward in Dublin accord with a holistic approach to water-resource management that seeks to link social and economic development to the conservation of natural ecosystems. The four principles say that (1) water is a limited and fragile resource that is essential for the maintenance of life, development and the environment. Water (2) should be developed and managed on a participative basis and users, planners and politicians should be involved at all levels. Women (3) play a central role in the provision, administration and maintenance of water, which (4) has an economic value in all competing applications and should be recognized as a valuable asset.

Shortly after their approval, the Dublin principles were adopted by the United Nations Conference for Environment and Development in Rio de Janeiro. In *Agenda 21* (Chapter 18.8) water is designated as a 'social and economic asset', which is an extension of the fourth Dublin principle. Of course social aspects of water were already acknowledged in the other three Dublin principles, and they should be interpreted in association with each other and not, as can happen, in isolation. That is the only way to insist on the significance of water as an ecological asset and natural resource as stressed both in the Dublin principles and in *Agenda 21*.

As early as 2000, with Millennium Development Goal 7 (MDG 7) in respect of ecological sustainability, UN member States undertook to ensure that the proportion of human beings without access to clean drinking water would be halved by 2015. At the Rio + 10 Summit in Johannesburg in 2002, the requirement was extended to include sanitary facilities. Current forecasts agree that neither of these objectives will be reached. Fundamentally, however, the human right to water goes beyond those aims, since it provides for universal access to water and not a reduction by half of the number of people without clean drinking water and sanitary facilities.

Since governments have become increasingly aware of their own and mutual vulnerability, water as a theme has also acquired an unassailable place on the global political agenda. It is noticeable, however, that the focus in this regard has been shifting from intergovernmental politics to processes of global governance which include non-governmental actors such as transnational companies, institutions and NGOs. In Johannesburg, in 2002, not only regular intergovernmental conventions (of type 1) but agreements with the private sector and actors in civil society were included in the official UN-Summit results as 'type-2 partnerships' for the first time. Voluntary private initiatives were even to the fore at the 'Rio + 20' Summit. The magic formula was 'green economy' (or 'green economies'), in the sense of industry voluntarily assuming responsibility for environment and society and saving essential commodities such as water.

V Global partnerships

Scientific research into international policy offers a critical assessment of the extent to which new forms of taxation and economic measures are capable of solving growing problems associated with the destruction of the environment and resources – and of the democratic implications of self-imposed 'voluntary' economic commitments. I have used the EU initiative *Water for Life* (EUWI), with its four regional components (Africa, Latin America, the Mediterranean area and countries in Eastern Europe, the Caucasus and Central Asia), as a case-study for studying questions of the effectiveness and democratic legitimacy of public–private partnerships.[23]

It was been shown that type-2 partnerships, as approved in Johannesburg, do actually provide an opportunity for effective and legitimate global governance. Non-governmental actors have contributed the necessary new expertise, whereas governmental actors remain the driving force, which has largely guaranteed the democratic legitimacy of the initiatives in question. Nevertheless, the partnerships encountered real limits in the water sector. There was a decisive deficit in that they were restricted to the direct actors in the sphere of water: in other words, to private water-supply companies and NGOs particularly concerned with water questions. But water users and polluters such as farmers (in particular) were not included systematically. But without their readiness to commit to change, voluntary instruments can only take effect sporadically. The partnerships could not generate any fundamental change.

VI Social entrepreneurship

Currently, many people are setting their hopes on 'social entrepreneurs'.[24] In Rio, too, several events were concerned with this phenomenon, which is admittedly not new but increasingly the focus of awareness and interest. Social entrepreneurs are committed individuals who bring innovative entrepreneurial solutions to bear on social and ecological problems. My research group GETIDOS (*Getting Things Done Sustainably*) at Greifswald University in Germany investigates their potential for solving water problems. On an international level, Ashoka, a non-profit organization, has had a decisive influence on the phenomenon of social entrepreneurship. To date it has helped more than 2500 committed individuals worldwide to implement and develop their ideas. In recent years it has been joined by several other promotion organizations, such as the Skoll Foundation, the Schwab Foundation and Echoing Green.

Examples of entrepreneurs in the water sector commended by Ashoka are the Kenyan David Kuria with his 'Iko toilets', which are clean public lavatories and showers refinanced by user charges; the Ecuadorean Marta Echavarria, who finances water protection by voluntary contributions from those responsible for pollution; and the Indian Laxman Singh, who made his drought-ridden home region bloom again by means of a sophisticated rainwater collection or rain-harvesting system based on old traditions. In Europe, commendations have been received by, among others, the Slovakian Michal Kravcik who used decentralized projects to hold back the building of a large dam, and Roberto Epple, a Swiss citizen resident in France, who founded the European River Network.

VII Michal Kravcik: water for climate change

The excessive use of water resources, especially by agriculture, is still being countered merely by a reactive rather than a preventative approach. Regional or seasonal bottlenecks in supplies are tackled with, e.g., barrage projects, river diversions or water tankers to cover certain areas. But these are seldom long-term solutions. Anyway, they tend to alter seriously and even destroy existing ecosystems – usually with disastrous results, not only ecologically but socially and economically.[25]

For some time now there has been particular resistance to building barrages. At the beginning of the 1990s, when the government of Slovakia announced plans for a large dam in Tichy Potok on the upper reaches of the Torysa in the East of the country, the social entrepreneur

Michal Kravcik, together with his NGO 'People and Water', organized local communities to resist the construction. They not only protested but offered an alternative proposal, a new idea propagated later by Ashoka. This 'blue alternative' provided for communally-owned and decentralized renaturalization as well as large-scale reforestation projects. The main idea was not to draw off water as fast as possible by means of expensive underground channel systems, but to retain it in town and country to ensure its availability to the ecosystem, obviate the introduction of long-distance supply systems, and try to provide a cooling effect or air-conditioning by local evaporation. In this connection, Michal Kravcik stressed the traditional acquaintance of local farmers with rainwater collection and storage. In the meantime he also worked with the government of Slovakia for extensive implementation of his alternative proposal. He also promotes his 'climate cooling' concept at international conferences.[26]

VIII   Roberto Epple: Big Jump

Roberto Epple's commitment to water conservation and management started with protests against building reservoir dams. A broadly-based civil-protest movement at the end of the 1980s succeeded in doing more than delay the construction of new dams on the Loire in France. Alternative flood-prevention and flood-management measures, especially the establishment of inundation or flood-plain areas, anticipated measures which, with the Water Framework Directive, have become the water-policy guidelines of the European Union (EU).

The Water Framework Directive of 2000 gives the EU a future-oriented form of water legislation. Unfortunately the member States have not put it into practice, or have implemented it only inadequately. In order to inform as many people as possible of the mere existence of the Water Framework Directive, together with the European River Network Roberto Epple, the social entrepreneur, organized a 'river-bathing day' throughout Europe. During the 'Big Jump' hundreds of thousands of people all over Europe jumped into their rivers, to demonstrate the need for cleaner water before the public and politicians. Epple is convinced that getting into a river will help you to see it differently and appreciate it anew. If you were to bathe in your river, would you go so far as to drink the water? As a social entrepreneur, he is not concerned to pillory environmental offenders but instead wants them to work with him to protect freshwater reserves.

In Greifswald we have been studying Epple's approach as a socio-ecological experiment. We jumped into the local river, the Ryck, in July 2010 and 2011, in the context of a Big Jump involving questionnaires, media evaluations and water-quality assessments. The surveys had already shown that many people in Greifswald felt quite 'at home' on the Ryck, but 'hadn't been told much' about river management. Unfortunately, we also discovered that the Big Jump both rather reduced the inclination of many of those taking part, or looking on, to do something for the river, and that they had no idea of what might actually be done anyway. The EU Water Framework Directive does in fact call for public participation in tackling the Ryck too, but the responsible authorities of the Federal Land of Mecklenburg-Vorpommern (where Greifswald is located) are overburdened. They don't see that the river is more than a storm and rainwater drainage channel, that the endangered *Batrachospermum gelatinosum* (Red Algae) is found here, and that attempts are being made to re-establish migratory fish species such as sea trout. There would seem to be a long way to go, and a fundamental change would seem to be called for, before rivers are once again truly valued by the people and authorities on the spot and water resources are managed sustainably.

IX   Global thinking, local action

In order to protect the environment effectively, individual and collective, voluntary and compulsory activities must operate in concert. While environmental protection and sustainable life-styles are to the fore in public debate at the moment, to date there has been no real sign of a comprehensive changeover to a sustainable society. The stress is still on questions of individual behaviour and voluntary measures. To a considerable extent, all this talk of best practice and so on to be achieved by social entrepreneurship deflects attention from the actual state of the environment. A comprehensive, proactive policy is missing. For instance, even the German Government has stated that the EU Water Framework Directive will not be implemented by 2015 as scheduled, instead of taking the initiative and setting a good example. The Land Office for Environment, Nature Protection and Geology in the German province of Mecklenburg-Vorpommern is even working on the basis of a second and third deferment, and intends to leave it to future generations to restore the heavily impaired water resources of the area, such as the River Ryck in Greifswald. Meanwhile, directives on water conservation, such as those concerning the width of bank-protection strips, are being modified.

Although the media favour the image of Germany as an exemplary instance of international environmental policy, the situation is not so rosy as far as the actual quality of our water resources is concerned. Nevertheless, the commitment of individual social entrepreneurs, and especially that of many dedicated people on the ground, has produced a lobby for the environment, and accordingly for future generations. Personally, I put the emphasis increasingly on the social dimension of environmental policy: that is, on governance by local social relations. In their own common interest people produce social choice mechanisms[27] that also contribute to the protection of water resources. By virtue of international conventions, common standards, cooperation, trust and reciprocal ties can replace global hierarchies and markets. What we need is a system with units that are primarily determined by function and social significance, and are locally anchored yet simultaneously function in a global network through knowledge-based relationships. We have to think globally and act locally. A process of far-reaching changes is called for, and each of us jumping into our nearest river might well get it going.

Translated by J. G. Cumming

Notes

1. J. L. Lozán (ed.), *Warnsignal Klima: Gesundheitsrisiken: Gefahren für Menschen, Tiere und Pflanzen: Wissenschaftliche Fakten*, Hamburg, 2008, p. 5.
2. S. Postel, 'Die Süsswasserökosysteme schützen!', in: Worldwatch Institute (ed.), *Zur Lage der Welt 2006: China, Indien und unsere gemeinsame Zukunft*, Münster, 2006, pp. 112-47.
3. UNICEF (ed.), *UNICEF-Report 2012: Mein Recht auf Wasser*, Frankfurt, 2012.
4. J. L. Lozán, *op. cit.*, p. 6.
5. www.virtuelles-wasser.de, 30 April 2012.
6. A. Sonnenberg, A. Chapagain, M. Geiger & D. August, *Der Wasser-Fussabdruck Deutschlands: Woher stammt das Wasser, das in unseren Lebensmitteln steckt?*, Frankfurt am Main, 2009; www.waterfootprint.org/Reports/Sonnenberg-et-al-2009-Wasser-Fussabdruck-Deutschlands.pdf, 30 April 2012.
7. UNESCO (ed.), *Water a shared responsibility: The UN World Water Development Report 2*, New York, 2006, p. 2.

8. *Ibid.*, p. 393.
9. A. Sonnenberg *et al.*, *op. cit.*, p.11
10. W. Sachs & T. Santarius, *Fair Future: Ein Report des Wuppertal Instituts Begrenzte Ressourcen und globale Gerechtigkeit*, Munich, 2005, p. 111.
11. U. E. Simonis, 'Wasser: Knappheit vermeiden, Verschmutzung vermindern', in: G. Altner *et al.* (eds), Jahrbuch Ökologie 2012, Stuttgart, 2012, pp. 165–73.
12. Münchener Rückversicherungs-Gesellschaft, *TOPICS GEO. Natural catastrophes 2010: Analyses, assessments, positions*, Munich, 2011, p. 43.
13. S. Postel, *op. cit.*, p.120.
14. CIPRA International (ed.), *Water in Climate Change*, www.cipra.org/de/alpmedia/dossiers/23, 12 January 2012.
15. U. E. Simonis, *op. cit.*, pp. 165–67.
16. N. Carter, *The Politics of the Environment: Ideas, Activism, Policy*, Cambridge, 2007, p. 242; M. F. Giordano, M. A. Giordano & A. T. Wolf, 'International resource conflict and mitigation', *Journal of Peace Research* 42 (2005), pp. 47–65.
17. T. L. Anderson & P. Snyder, *Water Markets: Priming the Invisible Pump*, Washington DC, 1997.
18. M. Finger & J. Allouche, *Water Privatisation: Transnational Corporations and the Re-Regulation of the Water Industry*, New York: Spon Press, 2002.
19. UNESCO, *op. cit.*, 420.
20. K. Conca, *Governing Water: Contentious Transnational Politics and Global Institution Building*, Cambridge, MA, pp. 215–55.
21. I. Winkler, *Lebenselixier und letztes Tabu: Die Menschenrechte auf Wasser und Sanitärversorgung*, Berlin, 2011 (Download: http://www.institut-fuer-menschenrechte.de/uploads/tx_commerce/essay_lebenselixier_und_letztes_tabu_01.pdf).
22. L. Partzsch, *Global Governance in Partnerschaft: Die EU-Initiative Water for Life*, Baden-Baden, 2007.
23. L. Partzsch & R. Ziegler, 'Social entrepreneurs as change agents: a case study on power and authority in the water sector', *International Environmental Agreements* 11 (2011), pp. 63–83.
24. S. Postel, *op. cit.*, pp. 41–76.
25. L. Partzsch & R. Ziegler, *op. cit.*.
26. R. Lipschutz, 'From Local Knowledge and Practice to Global Environmental Governance', in: M. Hewson & T. Sinclair (eds), *Approaches to Global Governance Theory*, Albany, 1999.
27. R. Lipschutz, *op. cit.*, pp. 259–83, esp. p. 275.

'My God, it's our river, shouldn't we preserve it? Without the river, what else have we got?'

SYLVIE SHAW

1 Introduction

The Brisbane River coils its way through the heart of Queensland's capital city. Mud-brown in colour, it is a tidal river, lined with mangroves and tall rain-forest trees in the city's outskirts, but increasingly in urban areas, the river is shadowed by high-rise apartment buildings and more intensive housing as people seek a connection with the river through water views. However, the desire to be close to the river has had other untoward consequences. Rapid urban development has led to the widespread clearing of bush-land along the river in the cityscape and upstream; this has affected water quality in the river, and downstream in Moreton Bay, an embayment known for its iconic species of dolphin, dugong and turtles.

This article provides an overview of research into river users' perceptions and experiences with the Brisbane River. In qualitative interviews with residents in four sites along the river (rural, peri-urban, urban and coast), people described how much the river meant to them. Meanings are framed and located within a complex, multi-faceted relationship with the waterway and nature generally, in which physical, sensory, cognitive and spiritual experiences interact with cultural representations of the river as the life-blood of the river valley. In all, 40 interviews were conducted to examine the attitudes of residents about the river, its environs and water quality, and to document their subjective experiences of connection, including the spiritual, with the river environs.

Interviewees were chosen by selective sampling. Their ages ranged from 20 to mid-70s; over two-thirds were Christian (Anglican, Catholic, Pentecostal, Uniting and Mormon); around 20 per cent expressed 'no religion', while the rest comprised a smattering of other religious and spiritual faiths. The study builds on my previous research into people's connections to marine waterscapes, in an outpouring of what I term 'deep blue religion' which honours the sacred relationship between human and ocean manifested in a deep conviction of the importance of ocean care.[1]

II Water connections

At present there is limited research in Australia into people's social and spiritual connections to water-courses, and especially into the psycho-social and spiritual values which users attribute to rivers and watersheds in Queensland.[2] Local studies of the symbolic value of rivers have largely focused on Indigenous issues,[3] but, in Australia and overseas,[4] more research is being carried out into the socio-cultural understanding of waterways as the emphasis on water security issues increases.

Water is the very essence of life. It flows through the human body and the body of the earth. It acts as a source of purification, healing and communion with the divine. According to Mircea Eliade, 'water symbolizes the whole of potentiality; it is the *fons et origo* [source and origin], the source of all possible existence'.[5] Encased in the river's flow, water, or as Eliade puts it, 'living water', becomes a sacred symbol of eternal life, fertility and regeneration. Water is at the heart of religious worship, and one of the interviewees, a Buddhist, said that water 'washes your sins away. We also do ceremony for the spirits of the river. The spirits of the river need to be taken care of'. A Uniting Church member reflected on the sacred role of water in baptism, seeing the river as 'alive' and 'a place of new life', while a spiritual practitioner referred to the 'calming feeling that comes from the water', then added: 'Like any waterway, it's been subject to the misuse and mismanagement of humans for however long, but we're waking up to that and slowly changing how we approach it.'

III Approaches to the river

This study is based on the proposition that increased development, housing density, ecological strain and busy life-styles reduce people's capacity to connect with the river. Nevertheless, although they do not visit the river as much as they did in their childhood years, they still care for it. Regardless of the age or gender of the interviewees, many explained that the river played an important role in their lives. Whether they were newly-arrived or long-term residents, whether they lived on the river or travelled to and from work in the local ferry known as the 'City Cat', and whether they visited the river regularly or not much at all, most would agree that the river plays, or has played, a significant role in their lives. One of the interviewees who lives in an apartment overlooking the river explained: 'The river is integral to my life. I fell in love with Brisbane and fell in love with the river; it's so beautiful. I love waking up in the early morning and watching the life on the river, the river boats and the constantly-moving pageant of humanity…Everything I do is river-focussed.'

The river is also central to the health of the watershed and the sea downstream, but when interviewees talk about the river, their focus is not on ecological or habitat issues, but on their deeply personal connections with the riverway. They discuss their love for the river and the calming and peaceful feeling it gives them. It is a place 'to meditate, to meet friends, and a sense of community is important'. They mention how proud they are of the river, how the river centres them spiritually before going to church, how it encourages them to reflect on their lives, and how they relate to the river as part of God's creation. For many interviewees, regardless of their religious outlook, the river inspires thoughts of the spiritual. They may not use explicit religious or spiritual language to describe their experiences, but they comment, often with a sense of puzzlement, about the strength of their connection and the deep feeling it evokes: 'It's something I can't really explain', they say, or 'It's kind of like meditation I guess'.

The river offers an opportunity to appreciate the beauty of nature and to escape from the world. This has been the experience of a Catholic social justice advocate: 'Often when I'm feeling overwhelmed, I go for a walk or go rowing, very early in the morning. I believe the river and the beautiful big old trees along the bank have contributed a lot to my own sense of peace and inner strength during challenging times of my life. This is the place I escape to, to seek solace and to regenerate.'

Another interviewee said: 'I don't think I'd be as calm if I didn't go fishing on the river. That would be bad for my well-being, or at least my wife would think so'. In a busy city like Brisbane, with its rapid development and consequent reduction of green amenity, the river affords a place to relax, and these times are seen as therapeutic, serene, and tranquil. The river is regarded as 'life-giving' and 'soul-sustaining' in a spiritual sense, for 'there's always something to enjoy' there.

IV The research context

Research into which environments people find personally sustaining shows that they prefer natural to built environments, partly because of the restorative benefits such places offer.[6] Experiences in natural environments, particularly aesthetic places like the Brisbane River, give rise to positive outcomes in health, well-being and quality of life. The benefits are physical, emotional and psychological, and include a reduction in stress and mental fatigue,[7] an enhanced sense of peace and renewal, and fewer stressors related to poverty and housing density in inner-city environments.[8] Informants in studies of spiritual experiences in natural settings, particularly wilderness and forest environments, recall a deeper connection with God or a sense of transcendence beyond the self.[9] This finding is highlighted by studies of people's experiences in wild river systems, which document feelings of awe and wonder, an appreciation of the beauty of nature, an experience of serenity, and a deepening concern about encroaching development and its impact on the river and its surroundings.[10]

Most studies of the links between spirituality and nature experiences have been located in wilderness rather than urban environments. Spending time in wild places promotes an enhanced physical, emotional, intellectual and moral-spiritual outlook[11] and is a source of personal transformation and insight.[12] Nevertheless, the ecopsychologist Robert Greenway warns us that wilderness areas may begin to suffer from overuse.[13] If the wilderness is categorized as a place of personal transformation, it may become just another commodity unless people engage in wilderness preservation as well as self-preservation. This is timely advice. One possible solution is to revitalize and 'remystify' the cityscape. Randy Haluza-Delay's advice is that: 'To remystify the city we need first to break the association of nature with majestic mountains or pristine forests. The natural world does exist in the everyday lives of city dwellers, and wild nature close to home begs to be explored...The first step in remystifying the city is simply to look around'.[14]

This advice was taken seriously by one of the river-connected interviewees. Pagan by inclination, she is active in river regeneration work and enjoys watching the passage of life along the riverbank: 'There is a stretch of the river where you can get down close to the water; there is a sort of cave with rocks reaching out into the river, and in the afternoon there are always cormorants, seagulls, and other birds fishing, resting, and drying their wings. I've even seen a pelican and marvelled at how far down the river it must have flown or swam. I climb down this place to watch the river drift by. The soul in this piece of earth so close to the water seems sacred. I dip my feet in the water, sometimes small guppies nibble my toes, and I wonder at the vast world beneath the river's glazed surface: bull sharks, maybe gropers? At sunset it's a fiery wonderland! The setting sun's flame is reflected onto the river and funnily enough, in the broken glass left by teenagers on hot secluded dates.'

There is enchantment in this riverscape, even in the midst of the city. Haluza-Delay contends that remystifying the city opens up the kinds of possibilities encountered by this interviewee. Such experiences, he says, 'reawaken a sense of wonder and...alert ourselves to the marvels in familiar things', even the glittering broken glass at sunset. These events instil 'a compassionate sense of place that consciously links care of self and the broader world, both human and non-human.' Thus, from the viewpoint of compassion for place, a reduction in green space can affect a community's well-being, and certainly, all around this river city, green and treed spaces are under pressure.

V   Perceptions of change along the river

The removal of trees to make way for increased housing is in total contrast to the experiences of the first settlers, who were overawed by the lushness and fecundity of the river valley, finding it 'a veritable garden of Eden'.[15] John Oxley, an early explorer, was so affected by its beauty, and the colour and diversity of plant life, that 'it took his breath away'.[16] From the giant trees hung vines and creepers of every description, staghorns by the thousands jostled for space with the wild passion flowers. Here and there extra dark green patches of palms and giant fern forests were sprinkled with the delicate colours of thousands of orchids. On the river itself Oxley's boat glided through millions of pink and white water lilies.

Contrary to this description of heady and overwhelming beauty, one interviewee said that if people fell into the river these days 'they would need to have a hepatitis B injection' as the water seemed so polluted. She is saddened by the changes she has witnessed in the past 50 years but reports feeling powerless to do anything to halt the decline. She reminisced about her childhood growing up along the river, when people would flock to the local bathing pools, which were enclosed by fences as a protection against sharks. Another long-term resident mentioned the river's population of bull sharks as something to fear, but he added that, as children, they would dare one another to swim out to the river's centre: 'There were always bull sharks in the river. These are very aggressive snub-nosed sharks that are now infamous for taking dogs, and sometimes people, in the canals on the Gold Coast [an area south of Brisbane]. We little boys would dare each other to jump into the river at night from the water skiers' pontoon and swim out into the middle of the river and back again. It was like walking, or in my case, running, on water'.

He is still a deeply religious Roman Catholic, continues to regard the river as God's sacred creation, and enjoys recounting his childhood adventures on the water. When he was growing up in the 1950s, 'Hobos used to live in shacks along the river; they were built on stilts and had rickety wooden ramps running out to them. They used to tie their small row boats to these ramps and survived by catching fish and crabs. We little boys thought it was fun to sneak up at night and throw rocks on the shack roofs, and untie their boats and run off. Needless to say, they took a dim view of this and would lie in wait for us, trying to catch us, or just chase us off. We were quite safe as they were usually drunk on really bad alcohol.'

The hobos and jetties are long gone from the river but something else is missing too. For the past five years I have spent time exploring the remaining pockets of wild nature along the river in my local neighbourhood. Children rarely come here. Young children might visit these bush-land places with adults, but I rarely see children or teenagers riding their bikes, climbing trees, going fishing or adventuring. The majority of people are adults walking their dogs, exercising, or sitting watching the water. The outdoors, at least in this urban space, seems to be a place for adults, or adults with very young children, and the childhood exploits regaled by the interviewees have all but disappeared or have been replaced by tamer experiences, in manicured parks, shopping malls or behind computer screens.[17]

In Australia, as elsewhere, the amount of time people spend in the outdoors is decreasing and is being supplanted by indoor, often mediated experiences. This shift has important implications for physical and mental health. For instance, Australia's Mental Health Policy has established the need for research into interventions which can lessen the risks associated with life stress,[18] while several studies, both here and overseas, have shown that connecting to the natural environment, such as the river, can have positive health and well-being outcomes as well as being spiritually enriching and personally transformative.[19] A musician and spiritual practitioner depicts this well, using the river as a metaphor and likening the twists and turns in her own life to the river's serpentine movement and tidal flow: 'I know that I feel a strong connection to water and get restless if I'm grounded on land for too long. I am a sensitive and emotional person and I find the river soothing and comforting. Much like my own personality, there can be long stretches of smooth, still water and then suddenly, there are intense bends and twists along the way'. A Uniting Church minister also commented on the significance of the river's flow, and saw the movement of the water as 'metaphorical for God, and like God...beyond words'.

VI   Reconnecting to the river through river care

The interviewees' affinity with the river is palpable. The way the river frames their identity, or the way they feel when they connect with the water, is vitally important for some of them, so the next question was how to react if the river began to die, or the quality of its water became severely polluted. Several described it as 'a kind of death in the family', and would mourn its passing. An environmental educator lamented: 'I would feel like there would be a hollow or hole in my life'. Others said that they would miss it 'like an old friend'. Their concern for the river has galvanized some interviewees to join river-care projects, replanting native vegetation along the banks and protecting the trees from residential developments advertising 'river views' (and even 'river glimpses'). Those active in river-care display a simmering anger over what they perceive is a general lack of care for the river, the pollution and the rubbish. One looked to the future of the river as a stretch of water flanked by high-rise buildings, while another said: 'We don't have a right to degrade God's creation'. This view was echoed by several interviewees, and while not all see the river as religiously symbolic, many acknowledge that a spiritual or special reverence is present along the river. Another interviewee described herself as a 'lapsed Catholic' and her connection with the river as 'spiritual.' She explained why she was active in river-care: 'Rivers are actually the real life-blood. They're kind of the arteries of our lands, and they bring life. They actually enable life to happen. Without healthy rivers we're not going to have clean drinking water. If you don't have a healthy river, you don't have healthy water. Then there's whole ecosystems that are completely blown away, and yeah, it's death. I think humans, through ignorance, are the greatest enemy'.

These feelings of despair about the health of the river and the role of humanity in causing the problems are common perceptions. Overall, however, there is a general lack of awareness about the river, its health and water quality. Scientific studies of the river and of surrounding waterways across South-East Queensland show that the waterways are suffering. Each year, the scientific organization known as Healthy Waterways creates a 'report card' for the creeks, wetlands, and rivers in the region.[20] In 2011, the Brisbane River catchment regions received grades measured from C- to F, indicating the river system was in fair to poor health. In contrast, several interviewees, not aware of the river's health problems, were optimistic about the river's future, saying 'it's not as bad as it used to be', and especially noting the presence of bull sharks as an indicator of river health. Some commented on the river's brown colour, wishing it was as clear as in the past, but seemed unaware of the effects that years of clearing, dredging and changing habitat have had on the once clear pools that were interspersed along the river.

When I work with others pulling up weeds along the river, there is an ecological awareness about the place. The convenor of the local bush-care group tells me how crucial it is to keep a green corridor for the little brown birds, the 'LBBs' which are fast disappearing due to loss of habitat and attacks by feral animals, especially feral cats. 'We've got the big trees for the big birds but we've lost the under-storey, and we need to replace it'. Others mention the importance of the social connections they make by being involved in river-bank restoration, a point affirmed by studies of environmental volunteering.[21] Interviewees say that it restores their spirits, helps them cope with problems like depression and loneliness, and gets them into the outdoors and exercising. As a church bell chimes in the background, one of the volunteers, nominally an Anglican, remarks: 'This is my church'.

The river carers have a common sense of reciprocity for what they see as the rewards the river gives them. One of the younger volunteers told me that: 'Old Lady Brisbane can rest easy and not be too concerned about litter on the banks. I clean and prune her almost every day. There's coke cans, fast-food wrappers and fishing lines; plastic bags, juice bottles and aluminium foil. I take away the things that don't belong, and bring in their place things that do, by planting trees or bringing fresh compost from my garden. I will never disturb the wild-life here, just sit and admire it from a respectable distance, and I always bring my friends along for a bit of added company. Our relationship with the river is based entirely on reciprocity. I know that if this constant giving and taking did not exist, I wouldn't be rewarded as abundantly as I am. There is enlightenment to be found by the river'.

This notion of eco-altruism is common amongst river volunteers who have embraced a kind of river ethos and etiquette, and have integrated a river consciousness in the way they live their lives. Elan Shapiro, a habitat restoration worker, suggests that when individuals are involved in land restoration work, they not only feel a sense of well-being by connecting with other like-minded people, but feel restored by their connection with nature.[22] Shapiro says that being involved in 'environmental restoration work can spontaneously engender deep and lasting changes in people, including a sense of dignity and belonging, a tolerance for diversity, and a sustainable ecological sensibility'. Taking care of nature becomes a heartfelt process, and (according to Shapiro), volunteers 'often fall in love' with the places they care for.

VII A river etiquette

How we treat nature and how we treat the river need to be embodied, not only in an environmental ethic, but in an environmental or river etiquette, a code of conduct which promotes respect for the river in the hope of engendering a practical manifestation of river care. This awareness could be further developed as 'a charter of river care', a commitment that residents make to the river's health and life. This charter could be accompanied by educational programmes and river-centred events that promote the river and people's connection with it. The river already takes centre stage at the magical fireworks celebrations on New Year's Eve and during the annual spring-time Riverfire Festival, an event with a special significance for one of the interviewees: 'The river symbolizes change and getting back to a peaceful state. I gave birth the night of Riverfire. The year before I got married on the cliffs overlooking the river. That was a life-changing event; it symbolizes change and rebirth'. A conservative Christian by upbringing, the interviewee is 'almost in awe' of the river. 'There's a life-force flowing through everything, the light of Christ. It emanates from God, and if that didn't go through everything, it would all just fall to dust'.

VIII   Conclusion

The perceptions and experiences of the interviewees show a deep affinity with the Brisbane River. For some, this is apparent in feelings of psychological and spiritual well-being. This brief overview of research on people's connections to the river suggests the need for more detailed research into the values which river users assign to this major waterway and other watercourses across South-East Queensland, how they use and experience these places, and how they perceive the future of waterways in the light of on-going environmental change.

Acknowledgements: I wish to thank the University of Queensland for its support of the research study and Dr Michael Pearce for his research assistance.

Notes

1. S. Shaw, 'Deep blue religion', in S. Shaw & A. Francis (eds), *Deep Blue: Critical Reflections on Nature, Religion and Water*, London, 2008.
2. V. Strang, 'Turning water into wine, beef and vegetables: material transformations along the Brisbane River', *Transforming Cultures eJournal* 1 (2006), http://epress.lib.uts.edu.au/ojs/index.php/TfC/article/viewFile/258/247

3. S. Toussaint, 'Kimberley friction: complex attachments to water-places in Northern Australia', *Oceania* 78 (2008), pp. 46–61; J. Weir, *Murray River Country*, Canberra, 2009.
4. V. Strang, *The Meaning of Water*, Oxford, 2004.
5. M. Eliade, *Patterns in Comparative Religion*, London & New York, 1958.
6. T. Hartig, G. W. Evans, L. D. Jamner, D. S. Davis & T. Garling, 'Tracking restoration in natural and urban field settings', *Journal of Environment Psychology* 23 (2003), pp. 109–23.
7. C. Maller, M. Townsend, A. Pryor, P. Brown & L. St Leger. 'Healthy nature healthy people: "contact with nature" as an upstream health promotion intervention for populations', *Health Promotion International* 21 (2006), pp. 45–54.
8. F. Kuo, 'Coping with poverty: impacts of environment and attention in the inner city', *Environment and Behavior* 33 (2001), pp. 5–34.
9. D. E. Little & C. Schmidt. 'Self, wonder and God! The spiritual dimension of travel experiences', *Tourism* 52 (2007), pp. 107–16; K. Williams & D Harvey. 'Transcendent experiences in forest environments', *Journal of Environmental Psychology* 21 (2001), pp. 249–60.
10. H. W. Schroeder, 'Ecology of the heart: understanding how people experience natural environments', in: A. W. Ewart (ed.), *Natural Resources Management: the Human Dimension*, Boulder, CO, 1996.
11. J. Davis, *Psychological Benefits of Wilderness Experience: Research and Theory*, 2008, http://www.johnvdavis.com/ep/benefits.htm.
12. P. Heintzman, 'Nature-based recreation and spirituality', *Leisure Studies* 32 (2010), pp. 72–89.
13. R. Greenway, 'The wilderness effect and ecopsychology', in: T. Roszak, M. E. Gomes & A. D. Kanner (eds), *Ecopsychology: Restoring the Earth, Healing the Mind*, San Francisco, 1995, p. 135.
14. R. Haluza-DeLay, 'Remystifying the city: reawakening the sense of wonder in our own backyards', *Green Teacher* 52 (1997), http://www.greenteacher.com/articles/mystifyingeng.htm
15. R. Kidd, *Aboriginal History of the Princess Alexander Hospital Site*, Diamantina, 2000.
16. ABC [Australian Broadcasting Corporation], 'Oxley's Discovery of the Brisbane River', in: *Australia's Centenary of Federation*, April 19, 2001, http://www.abc.net.au/queensland/federation/stories/s270973.htm.
17. R. M. Pyle, 'Nature matrix: reconnecting people and nature', *Oryx* 37 (2003), pp. 206–14.
18. Commonwealth of Australia, .*National Mental Health Policy* 2008, http://www.health.gov.au/internet/publications/publishing.nsf/Content/mental-pubs-n-pol08-toc.
19. J. Pretty, 'How nature contributes to mental and physical health', *Spirituality and Health International* 5 (2004), pp. 68–78.
20. Healthy Waterways. 2011, *Report Card 2011: for the Waterways and Catchments of South East Queensland*, Brisbane, Queensland.
21. M. Gooch, 'Volunteering in catchment management groups', *Australian Geographer*, 35 (2004), pp. 198–208.
22. E. Shapiro, 'Restoring habitats, communities and souls', in: T. Roszak, M. E. Gomes & A. D. Kanner (eds), *Ecopsychology etc.*, op. cit., p. 225.

Water in the Old Testament

ERHARD S. GERSTENBERGER

I Introduction

Water is simultaneously a treasure of inestimable value and an incalculably dangerous threat. In one way or another all nations are menaced by tidal waves, tsunamis, torrential rain, floods and similar events. At some time we have all experienced the vital power of water, whether through a thirst-quenching mouthful lapped from a fresh spring, a relieving cold or hot bath, the scent of the earth and forest floors after long-awaited rain, the sap in crops coming up, murmuring brooks or dew on meadows in the early morning. Encounters with water have always been a fundamental aspect of existence for humans and for most forms of life. Life in the ancient East from which the Hebrew scriptures have come down to us depended on the water supply. When rivers were the sole source of this essential substance, as in lower Mesopotamia, human settlements relied on sophisticated irrigation techniques. Other strategies had to be developed wherever agriculture depended on the annual rainfall. Well-digging and the provision of cisterns were ways of guaranteeing a water supply.

Boats and fishing called for greater expanses of water, which in their turn promoted the human faculty of invention. The people of Israel came into being in the early first century, mainly in the mountainous area of the region later known as 'Palestine'. The coastal plain up to the Mediterranean and the present Arabian desert did not form part of the territory in which they actually settled, as little as the snowy heights of Lebanon. The ancient Israelites experienced water mainly in the form of rivers (the Jordan and its backwaters), lakes (Genezareth) and rainfall. It was non-existent or scarce in many places: in the hot months of the year dried-up river beds (wadis) lost all trace of moisture. Dry conditions were only too evident in the southern deserts (the Negev), and the extreme state of the deep Jordan Valley was unmistakable. But even in these border areas the ancient Israelites' experience of water remained highly-nuanced, variable and complex. Consequently, the Hebrew scriptures do not feature a uniform concept of water.

II Evil water

Of course the inhabitants of the ancient East considered and tried to decipher the origin and nature of water. Any such tremendous and cosmic force must, it seemed, be truly divine. But how did it relate to the divinities that were held to be responsible for the existential realm known as 'the world'? The destructive power of water appeared to conceal no more than death-dealing energy. Accordingly, at some time in the past the 'good' divinities must have mastered this chaotic force in order to make life possible. This idea implied a profound, seemingly irreconcilable opposition between creative powers and this murderous frenzy from the very depths of time. At first, in Israel, the general image of the primitive state of things, the sheer chaos redeemed by the creative order emanating from God's life, was somewhat vague and blurred: 'In the beginning when God created the heavens and the earth, the earth was a formless void and darkness covered the face of the deep (Hebrew, *Tehom*; cf. the name of the Babylonian goddess Tiamat), while a wind from God (*ruah* = "the spirit of God"?) swept over the face of the waters' (Gen. 1.1–2).[1]

Here it is already clear that God did not create the waters, which were present only as a primal force. The creation of all that is from nothing is a much later and very abstract concept derived from Greek philosophy. The primeval struggle between God and the chaos of the deep and its mythic personifications played a central role in Babylonian and Ugaritic myths,[2] but also in some biblical traditions: 'You divided the sea (Hebrew and Urgaritic = *jam*) by your might; you broke the heads of the dragons (Hebrew and Ugaritic = *tanninim*) in the waters. You crushed the heads of Leviathan (Hebrew and Ugaritic = *liwjatan*); you gave him as food for the creatures of the wilderness' (Ps. 74. 13f; cf. Ps. 77.17–20; Is. 51.9f).

The Enemy was called 'sea', 'dragon', 'Leviathan' and so on, just as in the Urgaritic myth of primeval struggle, but might also appear as a prince, judge or 'river' (*nahar*) and, in Psalm 93.3f for instance, was assigned the majestic plural *neharot* (possibly: 'river monster'):

> Yahweh, the rivers (*neharot*) raise,
> the rivers (*neharot*) raise their voices,
> the rivers (*neharot*) raise their thunders;
> greater than the voice of ocean (*jam*),
> transcending the waves of the sea,
> Yahweh reigns transcendent in the heights (cf. Ps. 96.11; 98.7f).

The ancient audience had to face the mortal force of the divinely conceived primeval waters. They did not speculate about the origin of the phenomenon. There was no point in discussing Yahweh, the Creator of the world, or his origin, for he assailed chaos, curbed the cosmic powers, and made life possible on the dried-up and then refreshingly re-irrigated earth. The demons of chaos had to give way, and acknowledge Yahweh's supreme power, and the floods even clapped their hands (cf. Ps. 98.8), for they were not simply destroyed and wiped out, but remained in existence and effective, even if within certain limits. This meant that the hostility of the primeval state of things was not considered to be totally 'evil' in the sense we find familiar. There was no dualistic mutual exclusivity of chaos and creation, but creation somehow integrated chaos. Admittedly, the monstrous floods had to serve life, for 'You set a boundary that they may not pass, so that they might not again cover the earth' (cf. Ps. 104.5–11). In the Babylonian Enuma Elish creation myth, the world is formed from the body parts of the slain primeval divinities. But still, in every water disaster, the forces of chaos can constantly threaten the orderly world. Here we encounter an unfathomable contradiction: the order of the world has to be wrested from the power of chaos, and God is victorious after deathly combat. Furthermore, the primal waters attain their life-preserving capacities in the form of a tamed heavenly ocean that bestows rain, and in that of a lower sea that ordains the groundwater level and can be tapped by means of springs and wells (cf. Gen. 26.15–22):

> You fixed the earth on its foundations,
> unshakeable for ever and ever;
> You wrapped it [the earth] with the deep (*tehom*) as with a robe,
> the waters overtopping the mountains.

At your reproof the waters took to flight,
they fled at the sound of your thunder,
cascading over the mountains, into the valleys...
You set springs gushing in ravines,
running down between the mountains,
supplying water for wild animals,
attracting the thirsty wild donkeys (Ps. 104.6–7,10–11).

At the same time they retain a destructive power which may be discharged against creation. In the biblical flood narrative, which is wholly in the tradition of ancient Eastern water disasters,[3] and certainly preserves experiences of gigantic catastrophic floods, God's anger sets off the process of destruction: 'In the six-hundredth year of Noah's life, in the second month, on the seventeenth day of the month, on that day all the fountains of the great deep (= *tehom*) burst forth, and the windows of the heavens were opened. The rain fell on the earth forty days and forty nights...And all flesh died that moved on the earth, birds, domestic animals, wild animals, all swarming creatures that swarm on the earth. And all human beings, everything on dry land in whose nostrils was the breath of life died' (Gen. 7.11–12, 21).

God's good creation is not all peace, harmony and sunshine. It has (contrary to the order desired by its considerate Creator?) a horribly dark side. Pointless destruction threatens whenever certain incomprehensible earthly circumstances prevail. The attribution of divine wrath to the excessive 'wickedness' of the human race, and the reference to the mythical union between the 'sons of God' and human females in Gen. 6.1–4, are inadequate attempts to account for the impenetrable nature of (divine) judgment. The ancient traditions of Yahweh's saving action when he sent the Israelites went up on dry land in the (Red) sea (Ex. 14f), and on Mount Tabor, or at Megiddo (Judges 4f; cf. 5.4, 19–21), refer in part to the notion of Yahweh as a weather god.[4] The chaotic underworld is a threat to life in the psalms of individual lamentation. Yet even in this genre the context of guilt is left quite open: 'The waters closed in over me; the deep (*nahar*) surrounded me; weeds were wrapped around my head at the roots of the mountains. I went down to the land, whose bars closed upon me for ever...' (Jonah 2.4–7; cf. Ps. 32.6; 69.2f.; 88.18).

Seen from our viewpoint, which is heavily influenced by abstract-monotheistic ideas, God has an ambivalent relation to the waters of chaos. The Creator God defeats the primeval powers and integrates them in the orderly world. They remain as a seething cauldron of potential disorder, and retain traces of their divine power, perhaps with the subliminal notion that the too smoothly ordered world needs an occasional incursion of destruction and a fresh start.

III Rain and spring

The ancients knew that even good water possesses a certain degree of self-will, and ultimately it is only the independent spirit of a tumultuous force held in restraint. That is why well-diggers chant their mysterious magical songs, as with: 'Spring up, O well!' (Num. 21.17), and 'the water of bitterness that brings the curse' can disclose dishonour and sin (Num. 5.16–22) and pure water can effect a ritual cleansing (Ex. 29.4; Lev. 6.20f; 11.40; 14.8; 15.27 *et al.*).

Sometimes there are hints of notions that spirits or demons inhabit water-courses (cf. Gen. 32.23–5) and are closely associated with the liquidity of the element. Water has its own potency but it also conforms to the will of God. He controls rainfall, makes springs burst forth, and can even (and magical notions are at work here too) make it possible for Moses to strike the rock so that water gushes out for the people to drink (Ex. 17.5–6; Num. 20.11).

Old Testament farmers were wholly dependent on a timely and adequate supply of water (primarily of rain), and incorporated this fact resolutely in their religious awareness. If the harvest came out well, God had to be thanked for his bounty in word and deed:

> You visit the earth and water it, you load it with riches;
> God's rivers brim with water to provide their grain.
> This is how you provide it;
> by drenching its furrows, by levelling its ridges,
> by softening it with showers, by blessing the first-fruits.
> You crown the year with your bounty (Ps. 65.9–12).

A precondition of a successful harvest is sufficient rainfall in winter and while corn, olive trees and vines are growing (cf. Hos. 2.7–10; Jer. 5.24; Deut. 11.14; Ps. 84.7), it has to be vouchsafed by God and possibly requested and made possible by regular religious rites. Drought was a curse for those living in the East. The inevitable question was what kind of failure might have provoked this form of punishment called down on us. Penitential services had to be held, as indicated in, say, Jeremiah 14.1–9. Humans and animals languished and were parched with thirst: '...the ground is cracked. Because there has been no rain on the land, the farmers are dismayed, they cover their heads' (v. 4). People pleaded with God (v. 7–9). Times of drought led to migration (cf. Ruth 1.1), for the lack of water could be mortal. But if God's loving-kindness and commendable human behaviour ensured a due balance of nature, the harvest was celebrated with great joy, especially during the three major feasts of the year (cf. Ex. 23.14–6; 34.18–26; Lev. 23.4–44; Deut. 16.1–17). The importance of dedicating the first-fruits of field and cattle to God and the needy was often stressed (cf. Lev. 19.5–10.23–5; 23.10–11,22ff). Such allocations formed part of various rites in the fields, in families and in sanctuaries.

The generously-watered plains between or on the periphery of mountain ranges (such as Jezreel, Sharon and the Jordan Valley), or high plains suitable for rearing cattle, such as Bashan, were ideal locations for a prosperous life. From the 'drier' perspective of the desert areas, Palestine seemed to be richly supplied with such pastures, was celebrated as the 'land where milk and honey flowed' and produced especially outstanding results in its vineyards (cf. Num. 13). But the fields might bring forth 'thorns and thistles' instead (Gen. 3.17–19), a condition which the ancient Israelites knew and experienced as a curse. Collective hope focused on rich vegetation: 'They shall come and sing aloud on the height of Zion, and they shall be radiant over the goodness of the Lord, over the grain, the wine, and the oil, and over the young of the flock and the herd; their life shall become like a watered garden, and they shall never languish again' (Jer. 31.12). Water even became a metaphor for one's existential condition. Balaam utters an oracle when he sees Israel camping tribe by tribe, and foretells a time when 'Jacob' will see 'Water... flow from his buckets, and his seed shall have abundant water' (Num. 24.5–7). The desert blooms if it is the will of God (Is. 41.18–20). The garden of Paradise is full and overflowing with water and provides a reservoir for the whole world (Gen. 2.8–17).

The agriculture of somewhat more distant towns also suffered from rapid and intensive fluctuations in the weather. A lack of rain pushed up the price of foodstuffs and emptied urban reservoirs. Every settlement needed access to or a store of fresh water. Jerusalem was no exception. Even before David there had been a water shaft in the Jebusite city (2

Sam. 5.8), and Hezekiah made a pool and a new underground conduit, and brought water into the city from a source outside the walls (it could not be located inside because of its divine occupant) (2 Kings 20.20). The inscription in that technical masterpiece, the Shiloh (Siloam) Tunnel, is still to be seen there (cf. TUAT II, 4, pp. 555ff). The narratives of the patriarchs and Moses, for example, show that the urban imagination was especially prone to dreams of rural idylls, and the spring or well was seen as a scene for romantic love (cf. Gen. 29.1–14; Ex. 2.16–21). God's presence is mysteriously amalgamated with the water of the source; malicious water makes an appearance in the Song of Songs: 'Many waters cannot quench love, neither can floods drown it' (Song 8.7), and the good water (cf. Song 2.11ff) is to be found in the more comprehensive metaphor of the 'garden' (Song 4.12–6; 8.13). Nothing that humans need is so essential as water. A single draught is life-giving (cf. Judges 4.19; 15.18ff), but it must be a healthy drink (cf. Ps. 69.22; Ex.15.23, 25). Thirst is exhausting and deathly (cf. Ex. 17.3; Judges 15.18ff; Is. 41.17; Amos 8.13). There is no speculation about how water takes effect in the body before it is voided, or how its healing and cleansing virtues are exercised. It is sufficient to know that it gives, maintains and restores life in some mysterious way (cf. 2 Kings 5.10–14; Is. 41.18).

Accordingly, nature, humankind and God were conceived of as a union of forces. With regard to the moist element, humans certainly constituted the weakest part of the whole chain. God and water interacted at a higher level. But humans also had an active and a passive function in the interplay of forces. Their technical capabilities were called on actively in well-digging and ship-building (cf. Gen. 6.14–6; Ps. 107.23–32; 1 Kings 9.26–8), effective agriculture (cf. Is. 28.23–9), and possibly also holding back scarce water by building dams (cf. Proverbs 17.14; 1 Chron. 14.11).[5] In the passive mode, it was a question of ordering one's life before God so that a lack of rain or a flood sent as punishment could be avoided (cf. Lev. 26.18–20; 1 Kings 17.7; 18.1–4). In addition to hard labour on the land, humans were certainly also constantly responsible for many types of ritual, prayers and songs (as is still the case in many rural areas of the world).

IV Spiritualizations

There are two aspects to the ancient Israelites' conception of what might lie beyond existential reality. On the one hand, they clearly believed in a paradisiacal stage before the beginning of human history proper.[6] It possessed an abundance of water and luxuriant nature. The four primal rivers were sources of life for the entire globe (Gen. 2.10–14; cf. the reference to Jerusalem: 'On the holy mount stands the city he founded; the Lord loves the gates of Zion more than all the dwellings of Jacob, Glorious things are spoken of you, O city of God', Ps. 87.7; 36.9f). The 'garden' of Eden was blessed with fruitfulness in profusion, and accordingly it was scarcely labour-intensive. But sweat poured down in streams on account of the harsh reality, because the dry ground, which is 'cursed…because of you' could actually be 'mastered' only with toil and trouble (Gen. 3.17–19, cf. Gen. 1.28f). On the other hand, after death, in the underworld, people could look forward to 'sinking in the deepest swamp' and stepping into 'deep water' (Ps. 69.2–3, or expect 'water draining away' and 'lying in the dust of death' (Ps. 22.14–6). The lack of water, or the presence of water that was dangerous and unpalatable, made existence there down below insufferable, and calcified the body until it became a mere shadow of itself. Ideas of this kind can be found in the Middle East thousands of years before the appearance of Israel, as is shown in the numerous Sumerian–Akkadian tales of descent into the underworld and the miserable 'life' experienced there.[7] There was a sharp contrast between an ideal existence in paradisiacal surroundings and an existence (almost) entirely bereft of water in precarious circumstances. The inhabitants of the ancient world would have found a happy life without an adequate supply of water inconceivable.

Given the immense significance of water for life pure and simple, it is not surprising that the Hebrew word *majim* (a plural form) in the Old Testament is also used figuratively on occasion. In these cases the positive meaning is wholly to the fore, but the terrible danger of uncontrolled incursions of water and shapelessness may also be intended.[8] Humans may be as 'unstable as water' if they lose control of themselves (Gen. 49.4) and are tormented; their palates are 'drier than a potsherd', their tongues are 'stuck to their jaws', they 'drain away like water running to waste' and 'wither like trodden grass' (Ps. 22.15; 58.8). A warrior's heart may become 'like water' (Joshua 7.5). A less drastic effect is obtained by expressions such as [on the princes of Judah] 'I will pour out my wrath like water' (cf. Hos. 5.10) or the strong injunction 'let justice roll down waters, and righteousness like an ever-flowing stream' (Amos 5.24). Here the comparison relies only on the liquid nature of the element. 'Good news' may be like a cooling draught of water (Prov. 25.25) and words are sometimes like 'deep waters' (Prov. 18.4; 20.5). But the theological connotations of figurative language are more important in the present context. God himself is absolutely essential for life, just like the water we drink:

> As a doe longs for running streams,
> so longs my soul (Hebrew *nefeš*) for you, my God.
> My soul thirsts for God, the God of life;
> when shall I go to see the face of God? (Ps. 42–3.1–2).

This is a visualization of the Deity from a period when (even in Israel, it would seem) a statue of God in the Temple (the 'see' in v. 2 can certainly not mean anything else) represented that which was superhuman and invisible. It is no mere accident that the believer's 'soul' (*nefeš*) as it were provides the sounding-board here. *Nefeš* is the outcome of creation, the human creature originating in God's breath, that is one with the body, and yet can be seen as distinct from it, the 'dust of the ground' (Gen. 2.7). The divine presence, or community with God, is the goal of insatiable human longing, – or is God actually to be 'incorporated', or consumed, like water? God in his indispensability has the characteristics of water. He is or possesses the 'source' of life (Ps. 36.10; Proverbs 14.27; Jer. 2.13; 17.13). Living waters also come from Jerusalem, God's dwelling-place (cf. Ps. 87.7; Gen. 2.1–14).[9] It is scarcely surprising that one's entire relationship to God can be portrayed as a quest for the water that sustains life so wonderfully: 'The poor and needy seek water…' (Is. 41.17). This restriction to the lower social orders does bring a certain insubstantiality of the scene into play. It is stated more unequivocally in Amos: 'The time is surely coming, says the Lord God, when I will send a famine on the land; not a famine of bread, or a thirst for water, but of hearing the words of the Lord' (Amos 8.11, cf. v. 12).

The food which is absolutely life-sustaining is the word, Yahweh's instruction. The fundamental theological pronouncement on the theology of the word probably comes from the period in which the early Jewish community formed around the Torah. It is expressed in greater detail in Isaiah 55: 'Ho, everyone who thirsts, come to the waters'…For as the rain and the snow come down from heaven, and do not return there until they have watered the earth, making it bring forth and sprout, giving seed to the sower and bread to the eater, so shall my word be that goes out from my mouth; it shall not return to me empty, but it shall accomplish that which I purpose, and succeed in the thing for which I send it' (Is. 55.1–10f).

In accordance with this spiritualization of the discourse about water, Yahweh's community itself becomes an invigorating source: '...you shall be like a watered garden, like a spring of water whose waters never fail' (Is. 58.11). Thereafter the image makes an abrupt transition to become another (though parallel) notion of the community of Yahweh actively promoting reconstruction. Then the community acquires the new designation which makes rehabilitation possible: 'Your ancient ruins shall be rebuilt; you shall raise up the foundations of many generations; you shall be called the repairer of the breach, the restorer of streets to live in' (Is. 58.12; Hebrew: *goder pereṣ mešobeb netibot lašaebaet*).

What connotations does the metaphor of water (and nutrition) contribute to the 'word' of Yahweh? The most urgent necessity of the word is to the fore. Life is impossible without Yahweh's guidance. Furthermore, God is creatively active in his word. His teaching brings life and fertilizes 'the land', that is, the community. 'It does not return empty', for the word of God must give life (in cooperation with humankind, just as rain exerts a fertilizing effect on the cooperative earth: cf. *jld*, *ṣmh* [hif], 'bring forth' and 'sprout' as prominent expressions in Is. 55.10). In this theology the 'word' acquires an innate dynamism, as it clearly does in the prophetic tradition and in that of the Torah. It becomes a medium of divine action. The element of 'water' inherits a degree of expressive power from the long history of religion in Mesopotamia and is still effective in the Hebrew Bible.

Translated by J. G. Cumming

Notes

1. Claus Westermann's translation, *Genesis* (BKAT I.1), Neukirchen-Vluyn, 1974, p. 107.
2. Non-biblical sources are cited in accordance with Otto Kaiser (ed.), *Texte aus der Umwelt des Alten Testaments* (TUAT), Gütersloh, vols I–III, CD-ROM edition, 2005; cf. here: Wilfred G. Lambert, 'Enuma Eliš', in TUAT III, pp. 565–602, especially the victory over Tiamat, *ibid.*, pp. 583–7; Manfried Dietrich & Oswald Loretz, 'Der Baal-Zyklus KTU 1.2–1.6', in TUAT III, pp. 1091–198, especially Baal's defeat of the sea-god Yaam, *ibid.*, pp. 1118–34.
3. Cf. Karl Hecker, 'Das akkadische Gilgameš Epos', in TUAT III, pp. 646–744,

especially the flood narrative on cuneiform tablet XI, *ibid.*, pp. 728–38, and Wolfram von Soden, 'Der altbabylonische Atramhasis Mythos', in TUAT III, pp. 612–45, especially plague and flood on tablets II and III, *ibid.*, pp. 629–45.

4. Daniel Schwemer provides a comprehensive interpretation of the characteristics of Mesopotamian weather gods; cf. *id.*, *Wettergottgestalten Mesopotamiens und Nordsyriens im Zeitalter der Keilschriftkulturen*, Wiesbaden, 2001; cf. *id.*, 'Wettergott/Wettergötter' (2006), in: www.wibilex.de .

5. Cf. the plethora of discussions of water in the Palestinian context: Gustaf Dalman, *Arbeit und Sitte in Palästina*, 7 vols, 1928–42, here vol. 2: *Der Ackerbau*, Gütersloh, 1932 (reprint Hildesheim, 1987); Wiel Dierx & Günther Garbrecht, *Wasser im Heiligen Land*, Mainz, 2001.

6. The view can be substantiated that Genesis 3 is not an independent stage but only the necessary completion of the creation of humankind: how could people exist at all without the 'knowledge of good and evil'?

7. Cf. Willem H. P. Römer, 'Inannas Gang zur Unterwelt', in TUAT III, pp. 458–95; Gerfrid G.W. Müller, 'Akkadische Unterweltsmythen', in TUAT III, pp. 760–80.

8. Cf. Ronald E. Clements & Heinz-Josef Fabry, '*majim*', in ThWAT IV, 1982, pp. 843–66.

9. The image of the living water which may be God himself has a human sexual parallel in Proverbs 5.15–19: 'Drink water from your own cistern ...; ... rejoice in the wife of your youth .... May you be intoxicated always by her love' (cf. Song of Solomon 4.15).

Water as Sacrament
Global Water Crisis and Sacramental Stewardship

MARK J. ALLMAN

I Introduction

My daughter was given a *Noah and the Ark* play set last Christmas. As she marched pairs of plastic animals into the ark, I wondered who might think this toy was appropriate for children when the entire story was premised on God committing global genocide. The Noah's ark narrative may not be suitable for children but does serve as a modern morality tale. God finds humanity's sinful behaviour irredeemable, so God sends the great flood. The world today is facing a much slower, but no less destructive flood because of rising sea levels due to global warming caused by human behaviour. Like the story of Noah, this flood is the result of human sinfulness, but unlike the Noah tale, this flood does not come from the hand of God. It is a curse humans inflict on themselves and all of creation. The global water crisis is not limited to rising sea levels; it includes dire threats, especially to those who live in the developing world.

In this essay I shall explore the global water crisis theologically from a sacramental–ethical perspective. I shall examine the nature of water, the nature of a sacrament, and how a sacramental understanding of water can inspire Christians to become advocates of water justice. Notions of water as a sacrament may inspire Christians to work for water justice on the basis of the dual obligations of justice and sacramental stewardship.

II Water

The state of water is both tragic and paradoxical. Water covers nearly 75 per cent of the earth's surface, but only 3 per cent of it is fresh water and less 1 per cent of the earth's fresh water is accessible and usable by humans. That less than 1 per cent is enough to sustain the global population, but one billion people on the planet (one out of eight) do not have access to clean water. This results in 3.5 million deaths each year from water related illnesses, of which 84 per cent are children (approximately one child every 20 seconds).[1] The use and costs of water are also unequally distributed. For example, a person in the United States uses more water in a five-minute shower than a person in the developing world uses all day, and the urban poor often pay five to ten times more per litre of water than their wealthy neighbours in the same city.[2] The crisis is compounded by competing interests (agriculture, industry and domestic use); ineffective management by governments; increased efforts to privatize water supply and distribution; war and political instability; and a general lack of political will to address the crisis. Water is poised to be a (if not the) major source of international conflict for the next century, resulting in failed States, conflicts within and between States, famine, migration, and global economic pressures.[3]

Right or commodity?

One of the principal debates surrounding the global water crisis is whether water is a human right or a commodity. Water is a basic necessity for human existence, as are food, air, shelter and health care. Without water, people die. Thus classifying water as a human right seems accurate. But what is often overlooked in the 'human right or commodity debate' is that water requires infrastructure (purification and a delivery system) to be usable. Some of the basic necessities of human existence are readily available and freely distributed (air); others are labour-intensive and require infrastructure and labour (food, clothing, shelter, and health care). While water at first seems more like air in that it is often available free of charge (rivers, lakes, and rain), usable/potable water is not free. It requires expensive infrastructure and labour; as such, water is more like the other basic necessities that are treated as both rights and commodities. The Catholic Church's teachings on water reflect a more nuanced understanding of water as both a right and a commodity.

The *Compendium of the Social Doctrine of the Church* describes water as 'a gift from God,' to which 'everyone has a right' and decries treating water as 'just another commodity among many' or as 'merely an economic good.'[4] Pope Benedict XVI, on World Water Day 2007, clarified the Church's understanding of water by describing water as 'a common good of the human family' and 'an essential element for life'. He went on to say: 'Access to water is in fact one of the inalienable rights of every human.', which ought to be managed according to the ethical principles of subsidiarity, participation, and the preferential option for the poor.[5] It is important to note here that Catholic social teaching on water describes *access* to water as a right and decries treating water exclusively as a commodity, but does not preclude the privatization of water.[6] Instead it engages the Church's teaching on private property, which distinguishes between 'use' and 'ownership.'

The primary focus of this article is not on the ethics of water alone, which I have written about elsewhere, and is addressed by others in this issue of *Concilium*.[7] The focus here is on the intersection of water, ethics and sacrament. In Catholic social thought, water is both a *common good* (given by God intended for all to use) and a *material good* that can be privately owned, so long as 'access to safe water and sanitation for all' are guaranteed.[8] If the water crisis were simply about questions of access and sanitation, then this would be principally a matter of social justice. But water ethics spills over into sacramental theology because water is used in liturgy and sacrament. The global water crisis is redefining water's meaning. What was once a symbol of purification and life has for many become a commodity they cannot afford and a symbol of filth and death. This makes the global water crisis not only a social justice issue, but one of sacramental stewardship.

III Sacrament

In 'The Sacramentality of Creation and the Role of Creation in Liturgy and Sacraments', Kevin Irwin posits that liturgy is 'the actualization of the paschal mystery for the believing Church through an act of proclaiming and hearing the Word and celebrating sacramental rituals'.[9] In other words, sacraments are not only 'efficacious signs of grace, instituted by Christ and entrusted to the Church, by which divine life is dispensed to us',[10] they are a means of participation in the paschal mystery through symbols.

The ancient Christian maxim, *lex orandi, lex credendi* (the law of prayer is the law of belief) expresses a foundational concept in liturgical and sacramental theology, namely one can study what the Church believes by how the Church prays, for 'the Church believes as she prays'.[11] More recently, this maxim has been expanded as *lex orandi, lex credendi, lex vivendi, lex agendi* to express the notion that prayer and belief must influence not only how one lives day to day, but must also inform the social mission of the Church. But sacramental symbols cut both ways. The symbols are effective because they reflect, draw on, and parallel ordinary activities. 'For example, the use of water in baptism builds on the act of bathing, the use of bread and wine in the Eucharist presumes the act of dining, the use of oil in anointing of the sick supposes the human act of salving one's skin.'[12] This reflects the sacramental principle, namely that created things can be sources of grace (Rom. 19.20).

Irwin presents a sophisticated, sacramentally-grounded creation theology that: (1) distinguishes between two kinds of sacramental symbols: those that come directly from nature (water, fire), and those that derive from nature but are also the result of human ingenuity and labour (bread, wine, and oil); (2) attends to the relationship between the *symbols* that are used and the *words* that accompany their use, both of which require a response from the community that enjoys shared senses of meaning associated with the symbols and words; (3) recognizes that symbols are polyvalent (i.e., they have multiple meanings, as opposed to signs that tend to be viewed as objects with only one meaning), and that only some of the meanings are articulated verbally in the prayers.

Irwin concludes: '…the liturgical theology derived from symbols used in the context of the liturgy simply cannot concern "objects" alone. Nor can it refer to symbols, especially those from creation, simply as a means to experience God. To use creation in liturgy is to show reverence for creation through, with, and in which the incarnate God is disclosed and discovered. The use of material creation in the liturgy has traditionally been understood to reflect back to the Creator and to imply an understanding that rests on the sound foundation of theological anthropology.'[13] In the rest of his essay, Irwin describes how creation is used in contemporary liturgy. Nevertheless, his theoretical understanding of creation and sacrament can be applied to water as sacramental. But before I discuss water as sacrament, I wish to address another question of creation theology, viz.: 'Is creation the primordial sacrament?'

Creation as the primordial sacrament?

As visible and efficacious signs of God's grace, sacraments are not limited to the seven ritualized practices. Indeed, as Edward Schillebeeckx argued over 50 years ago, Christ is the primordial sacrament. More recently, *The Catechism of the Catholic Church* affirmed that the Church is a sacrament, albeit in an analogical sense.[14] Several theologians (Elizabeth Johnson, Dorothy McDougall and John Hart) have argued for an understanding of creation or the cosmos as the primordial sacrament. Such efforts attempt to counteract Christianity's anthropocentric and instrumentalist view of nature. Instead, they argue that creation has an intrinsic value; that it is a subject (not an object) equal in worth to humans; and that its value is not based on how it serves humankind. However well-intentioned, such efforts are problematical on at least three counts. First, these approaches run dangerously close to pantheism and panentheism (or, worse, idolatry) by blurring the distinction between creator and creation. Secondly, the category of 'cosmos' or 'creation' is too large a concept to be serviceable. The relational aspects of a creation theology are lost with such blunt categories. A sense of responsibility for the cosmos writ large is meaningless. One does not easily form an attachment to the whole of creation because one does not interact with the cosmos, only with its individual elements (plants, animals, rivers, mountains). If one of the aims of creation theology is to stoke a sense of ecological responsibility, then cosmic and creation theologies run counter to this aim. Finally, arguments about the 'primordialness' of sacraments are non-illuminative. Sacraments as instruments of grace and a means of participation in the paschal mystery cannot be quantified, just as grace itself is unquantifiable. Whether Christ, the Church, the cosmos or creation is the primordial sacrament is a distinction without a difference.

Therese B. DeLisio argues against cosmo-centric sacramental theologies in favour of a theo-centric sacramental theology or more accurately 'a Trinitarian theology of creation'.[15] She argues for an understanding of God as 'the one who is for, with, and within us and all of creation', which moves beyond traditional speculations on how the persons of the Trinity relate to each other and instead focuses 'on God's extra-relationality, that is, on who God is *pro nobis* – for us… [which] takes place in creation itself'.[16] For Irwin, creation is used in liturgy because it is the context of revelation. Similarly, for DeLisio, God's self-disclosure takes place within creation itself, whether it is the act of creation, the incarnation, the movement of the Spirit or a sacrament. There is no revelation apart from creation. By focusing on who God is *for, with, and within us* in the context of creation, DeLisio mitigates the dangers of anthropocentrism, while avoiding the pitfalls of pantheism and panentheism. DeLisio concludes: 'Taking a turn to the cosmos in sacramental theology means that we must seriously consider moving beyond the notion of Christ as primordial sacrament and opt, instead, for a more multidimensional and dynamic symbol of the Holy Mystery in our midst.'[17] Thus creation moves beyond mere object, but not so far as to become subject, nor is it reduced to a mere accident. Creation comes to be seen as the essential context of revelation. Drawing on this revered sense of creation, DeLisio argues that 'sacrament' is also a multi-dimensional term 'rooted in our multiple ways of experiencing God,' whereby sacrament as 'a symbol or action which points to, makes present, and facilitates participation in divine life' serves as a 'lens through which all of creation can be understood, interpreted, and appreciated as a material symbol of the very Mystery of God'.[18] Thus creation is the essential context of both revelation and sacrament.

IV Water as sacrament

Creation is used in liturgy not merely as a tool that reflects 'back to the Creator' or serves as a 'means to experience God'.[19] Creation is used in liturgy to show reverence for creation because it is the context of God's self-disclosure. Creation is revered because it is revelatory. This is particularly true of water.

Irwin's sacramentally-grounded creation theology is a useful hermeneutic for a theology of water as sacrament. First, his distinction between *symbols that come directly from nature* and *symbols that come from nature and human labour* does not easily apply to water. In the developed world, the ingenuity and labour behind water remain largely invisible. I turn on my tap and water flows. I think very little about the workers, piping and purification plants needed to make it available and potable. But for those who spend hours a day fetching water and collecting wood to burn so it can be boiled and purified, water is hardly free of human labour. Indeed, all of the symbols used in liturgy (water, fire, oil, bread, wine) are 'fruit of the earth and work of human hands', for none of them comes directly from nature. The fact that all sacramental symbols involve some form of human labour reflects the notion that God invites humans into a cooperative relationship, one in which the gift of creation alone is not a fitting offering because it would be giving back to God what has already been given.

Irwin's second point, that sacramental symbols and the words used in conjunction with those symbols require a response from the community based on shared senses of meaning, and his third point, that sacramental symbols are polyvalent and serve as a bridge between the sacred and the secular, can be conflated in a theology of water as sacrament. Sacramental symbols are effective because they parallel ordinary day-to-day activities. Ordinary objects become sacramental symbols because they are used in a communal liturgical setting (water becomes holy water and bread becomes the body of Christ). Ordinary activities become sacramental because of their association with liturgy (washing reminds us of baptism, eating becomes eucharistic). This is possible because the community shares senses of meaning regarding these objects in both the sacred and ordinary spheres. But the bridge goes both ways. How an object is used and perceived in day-to-day activities affects its ability to function sacramentally. What happens when the community's experience of the ordinary object renders it unfit, inappropriate or ineffective as sacramental symbol? This is especially true of water, the central symbol of baptism.

In baptism water is an indispensable symbol of new life, forgiveness of sin and membership in the body of Christ. But in the daily lives of one billion people, water is a deadly source of disease, polluted with excrement and chemicals; a commodity they cannot afford; or a staple that requires hours of labour. Polluted water, as John Hart notes, 'no longer has a sacramental character as a sign in nature of the Creator Spirit'. How can one baptize in water too filthy to drink? Water sullied with excrement and carcinogens is ineffective as a symbol for the washing away of the stain of original sin and in fact becomes a symbol of disease and death. Likewise, Hart notes, 'When water is *privatized*, its sacramental role in the commons is denied to many. Its availability as a sign of a loving Spirit who cares for all life is limited.'[20] How can one baptize in water so expensive it requires people to choose between buying the water needed for baptism or food and medicine? When water becomes an expensive commodity, it no longer functions as a symbol of

God's freely given redemptive grace; instead it symbolizes oppression and the commodification of grace.

Irwin encourages attending to both the use of sacramental symbols and the words that accompany their use. When the prayers in the Rite of Baptism for Adults, for example, are proclaimed in the context of the two-thirds world, the contrast is nothing short of tragic irony. The prayer of blessing of the baptism waters at the Easter Vigil (option A) recounts a host of biblical water images (creation, the great flood, the crossing of the Red Sea, the command to baptize all nations and the crucifixion) and speaks directly of the grace of water: 'In baptism we use your gift of water, which you have made a rich symbol of the grace you give us in this sacrament... By the power of the Spirit give to this water the grace of your Son, so that in the sacrament of baptism all those whom you have created in your likeness may be cleansed from sin and rise to a new birth of innocence by water and the Holy Spirit.'

The celebrant is instructed to stir the water either with the Easter candle or with his hand and say, 'We ask you, Father, with your Son to send the Holy Spirit upon the waters of this font. May all who were buried with Christ in the death of baptism rise also with him to newness of life.' The prayer speaks of how water both cleanses and gives new life, two properties that parallel the greatest challenges of the global water crisis: sanitation and access.

The instruction that the water should be moving/living water is also noteworthy. In nature, stagnant water is prone to disease; moving/living water is considered fresh. *The Didache*, one of the oldest Christian treatises (c. 90 CE), included the instruction that one should baptize 'in living water. But if you have no living water, baptize into other water; and if you cannot do so in cold water, do so in warm.'[21] The emphasis on living water is complemented by the general instruction directive that 'The water used in baptism should be true water and, both for the sake of authentic sacramental symbolism and for hygienic reasons, should be pure and clean' and that the font itself 'should be spotlessly clean.'[22] The general instruction also notes that immersion is the preferred method of baptism and 'If the climate requires, provision should be made for the water to be heated beforehand.'[23] Thus both words and actions of baptism reveal that water plays a sensual and indispensable part in baptism. The Church's theology of water is deep and rich, Trinitarian, and grounded in Scripture and tradition. This is all well and good for a theology of baptism, but symbols cut both ways. The greatest threat to the understanding of water as sacrament is not from any new theological movement or radical interpretation of Scripture. The gravest threat to water as sacrament and the practice of baptism comes from the state of water in the world.

V Conclusion: *lex vivendi, lex agendi*

The story of Jesus and the Samaritan woman at the well (John 4.1–42) is an apt allegory for the relationship between the one billion who are thirsty and the sacramentality of water. The Johannine philosopher Jesus employs the metaphor of living water and offers a treatise on salvation. The nameless woman is preoccupied with practical concerns. When he asks her for a drink, she is first concerned with how this will look (a Jewish man asking a Samaritan woman for water), then she points out that he has no bucket. Jesus promises: 'those who drink of the water that I will give them will never be thirsty' (v. 14). To which she replies: 'Sir, give me this water, so that I may never be thirsty or have to keep coming here to draw water' (v. 15), presumably because it would save her hours of work. This is a case of two people talking past each other. Jesus focuses on figurative thirst, while the woman is concerned with literal thirst.[24]

Likewise, if the Church today continues to focus its theology of water exclusively on theoretical and theological explorations of water's sanctity while ignoring the reality of the thirsty two-thirds world, it will soon find that this central symbol of the Christian faith has been redefined by environmental degradation, drought, and market forces. Symbols function because they tap into a community's shared senses of meaning. The meaning of water has changed. For many, it is no longer a symbol of new life and purification. This change forces sacramental and liturgical theology to turn to ethics, politics and economics. *Lex orandi, lex credendi, lex vivendi, lex agendi*.

The way water is used and talked about in liturgy can be a source for education on issues of water justice and for inspiring Christians to become advocates of water justice, not only out of a sense of charity for those who thirst, but out of a sense of sacramental stewardship. This can be done by using water more often in eucharistic liturgies by opting for the 'Rite of Blessing and Sprinkling Holy Water' instead of the Penitential Rite. The option includes three prayers for the blessing of the water, all of which speak of water as sacrament. The actual sprinkling itself should also be generous. Baptismal fonts (and holy water vessels at the doors of the church) should be clean, prominent and aesthetically pleasing. The use of water liberally and often, accompanied by prayers that speak of water as sacrament, stokes the imagination to see water a gift, a blessing and a source of life. These practices can be accompanied with raising awareness of the global water crisis through the Prayer of the Faithful, occasional sermons where appropriate (Sundays when baptisms are being celebrated) and by employing the 'Eucharistic Prayer for Masses for Various Needs and Occasions' that speak of water. The liturgical year also offers several opportunities for highlighting the material and spiritual importance of water: the Feast of the Baptism of the Lord, Epiphany, Sundays in Lent and Eastertide, the Rogation Days and other days devoted to creation, crops and rain. Church buildings can also serve as symbols proclaiming a creation theology that reveres water by fixing leaks, installing low-flow sinks and toilets, landscaping with native species that require no watering, using rain barrels and greywater, and reducing the amount of impervious surfaces to reduce water runoff. Finally, engaging in advocacy for global water justice (through such organizations as Catholic Relief Services and Caritas Internationalis) also becomes part of the liturgy for life and water.

Toilets and plants may seem out of place in a theology of water or beyond the pale for liturgy, but that is because liturgy is often celebrated as if the affairs of the world were irrelevant to the paschal mystery. Overly privatized or supposedly a-political liturgies are not merely unfortunate or misguided. They are forms of social sin because in not challenging the economic and political *status quo*, one that leaves a billion thirsty and kills 3.5 million annually, we are denying a cup of water (Matt. 10.42) to the one who cried out on the cross, 'I thirst' (John 19.28).

Notes

1. United Nations Human Development Programme, *Human Development Report 2006: Beyond Scarcity – Power, Poverty, and the Global Water Crisis*, New York, 2006; Water.org, 'Water Facts,' http://water.org/water-crisis/water-facts/water/; and Jie Lui, *et al.*, *Water Ethics and Water Resource Management*, Ethics and Climate Change in Asia and Pacific Working Project, Working Group 14 Report, Bangkok, 2011.

2. UNHDP, 10 and 35.
3. Office of the Director of National Intelligence (USA), *Global Water Security, Intelligence Community Assessment 2012-08* (2 February 2012), http://www.dni.gov/nic/ICA_Globalper cent20Waterper cent20Security.pdf.
4. Pontifical Council for Justice and Peace, *Compendium of the Social Doctrine of the Church*, Washington, DC, Nos. 484–5.
5. Benedict XVI, 'Message of the Holy Father Benedict XVI on the Occasion of the Celebration of World Water Day 2007', in Dennis Warner (ed.), *Catholic Social Principles Towards Water and Sanitation*, Baltimore, MD, 2009, pp. 11–12.
6. See Pontifical Council for Justice and Peace, 'Water, An Essential Element, An Update' (March 2006), http://www.vatican.va/roman_curia/pontifical_councils/justpeace/documents/rc_pc_justpeace_doc_20060322_mexico-water_en.html, nos. 2–6.
7. M. Allman, 'Theology H2O: The World Water Crisis and Sacramental Imagination', in T. Winright (ed.), *Green Discipleship: Catholic Theological Ethics and the nvironment*, Winona, MN, 2011, pp. 379–406. See also the following articles in this issue of *Concilium*: L. Partzsch, 'Water in Danger'; K. Lahiri-Dutt, 'Water Ethics'; and M. Barros, 'Life, Water and Liberation'.
8. Pontifical Council for Justice and Peace, *Water, An Essential Element, An Update*, No. 6.
9. K. W. Irwin, 'The Sacramentality of Creation and the Role of Creation in Liturgy nd Sacraments', in K. W. Irwin & E.D. Pellegrino (eds), *Preserving the Creation: Environmental Theology and Ethics*, Washington, D.C., 1994, p. 67.
10. *Catechism of the Catholic Church* (CCC), No.1131, http://www.vatican.va/archive/ENG0015/_INDEX.HTM.
11. CCC, no. 1124. As Irwin records (p. 67), the phrase '*lex orandi, lex credendi*' is a shortened version of '*legem credendi lex statuat supplicandi*', which is attributed to Prosper of Aquitaine (c. 390–455 CE).
12. K. W. Irwin, *op. cit.*, p. 70.
13. *Ibid.*, p. 73.
14. See E. Schillebeeckx, *Christ the Sacrament of the Encounter with God*, New York, 1963 and CCC, Nos. 774–6 and 780.
15. T. B. DeLisio, 'Considering the Cosmos as Primary Sacrament: A Viable Basis for an Ecological Sacramental Theology, Liturgy, and Ethics?', *Proceedings of the North American Academy of Liturgy* (2006), p. 172.
16. T. B. DeLisio, *op. cit.*, p. 172. See also K. Rahner, *The Trinity*, New York, 1970; K. Barth, *Church Dogmatics* I.1, Edinburgh, 1975. The literature on Trinitarian theology and creation is vast and beyond the scope of this essay, but see: L. Gilkey, *Maker of Heaven and Earth*, Garden City, NY, 1959; J. Moltmann, *God in Creation*, San Francisco, 1985; L. Boff, *Cry of the Earth, Cry of the Poor*, Maryknoll, NY, 995.
17. T. B. DeLisio, *op. cit.*, p. 174.
18. *Ibid.*, p. 174.
19. K. W. Irwin, *op. cit.*, p. 73.
20. J. Hart, *Sacramental Commons: Christian Ecological Ethics*, Lanham, MD, 2006, p. 80. Later he declares: 'Earth's waters have become less sacramental, less a revelatory sign of the Spirit's prescience and creativity, and more detrimental, more signs of human ignorance, carelessness, indifference, and greed' (p. 91).

21. "Concerning Baptism, *The Didache*, chapter 7, *Early Christian Writings*, P. Kirby (ed.), http://www.earlychristianwritings.com/text/didache-roberts.html.
22. International Committee on English in the Liturgy (ICEL), 'Christian Initiation, General Instruction', *Rite of Christian Initiation for Adults*, Chicago, 1988, Nos. 18–9.
23. ICEL, 'Christian Initiation, General Instruction', No. 20.
24. Sigríður Guðmarsdóttir, 'Water as Sacrament: The Samaritan Woman reflects on Liturgy and Justice', 26 January 2009, http://www.skr.org/download/18.589e653711f5b17101b800010351/Water+as+Sacrament+300109.pdf.
25. Cf. S. K. Perkins, 'Blessing Fields and Repelling Grasshoppers: Rogation Days in American Catholic Rural Life', in P. J. Rossi (ed.), *God, Grace and Creation* (College Theology Society Annual Volume 55), Maryknoll, NY, 2010, pp. 201–21.

'Give me this water...'
The Water of Life in John's Gospel

PIERRE LETOURNEAU

I Introduction

Water means life. This may seem pretty obvious, especially in over-developed countries where water is so abundant and so easy to find, that we swallow it without thinking. You have to be really thirsty to understand the mystery of water and to grasp its full symbolic meaning.

Mystics are utterly changed beings thirsting for God, and of course John, the mystic evangelist, is one of them. He made extensive use of symbolism in an attempt to convey to us, as far as possible, his intimate experience of the living God and of his Son Jesus, Saviour of the world. John uses numerous symbols in his theology, and the depth and extent of the symbolism of water give it a special place in his system. The well-known passage narrating Jesus' meeting with a Samaritan woman at Jacob's Well (John 4.1–42) is typically Johannine. It is particularly relevant to the theme of this issue of *Concilium*, and to what I want to say in this article, because it treats of thirst, water and, above all, the living water promised by Jesus. Of course this passage does not offer the only key to the meaning of John's water symbolism. We also have to consider, though less forcefully, what Jesus says on the final day of the Feast of the Tabernacles (7.37), as well as this gospel's account of the crucifixion (19.28–37)[1].

II Decyphering John

(a) *Theological DNA*

It is almost impossible to decode John's gospel without first picturing the two interwoven strands of the DNA, so to speak, which the author used to manipulate all the constituent elements of this literary work. The absolutely basic element of Johannine theology, God the Father, source of Life and principle of all salvation in the here-and-now and in the life hereafter, is always present between the lines, and less emphatically on the surface, of the account. Eternal life, an absolutely central theme in this gospel (cf. 20.30–1), is defined in terms of intimate knowledge of the one true God (cf. John 17.3).

But how can we know the Father so directly as to share in his life as God's children throughout all eternity (1.12–13)? Here we come upon the other strand of the Johannine narrative's theological DNA: the revelation of the Father *through the Son*. Indeed, this theme is all-pervasive, and I would have to cite the whole gospel to illustrate this other element of the controlling DNA proficiently. For my present purpose, it is sufficient to invoke the unparalleled words of the Prologue: 'In the beginning was the Word, and the Word was with God, and the Word was God... And the Word became flesh and lived among us, and we have seen his glory, the glory as of a father's only son, full of grace and truth...No one has ever seen God, [but] it is God the only Son, who is close to the Father's heart, who has made him known'[2] (1.1,14,18 [NRSV]).

The Jewish tradition inherited by most of the first members of John's community taught that God revealed himself to Moses (Ex. 3.14), who became God's exponent par excellence. By obeying the will of God revealed by Holy Scripture and the Law of Moses, the Jewish people would be assured of salvation (cf. John 5.39).

Obviously, there was nothing to prevent Christians of Jewish origin obeying the Law of Moses and believing in Jesus the Messiah, at least up to the point when Judaism was reorganized around the Pharisaic party after the destruction of the Temple by the Romans. The members of the Johannine community were to find themselves banished from the gathering in the synagogue because of their faith in Christ (*aposynagōgos* 9.22; 12.42; 16.2). Several of them, it seems, would chose to repudiate their Christian faith,[3] doubtless in order to re-enter the Jewish fold. The author of John's gospel undertook to write it in order to contain this destructive tendency, by demonstrating Jesus' incontestable superiority over Moses in revealing the Father (cf. 20.30–1). Moses was certainly a great prophet, and God's spokesperson, but Jesus is the divine Word who comes to us 'full of grace and truth' (1.17).

All the essential elements of this theological DNA are arranged appropriately in this superb definition of salvation: 'And this is eternal life, that they may know you, the only true God, and Jesus [the] Christ whom you have sent' (17.3).

(b) *Symbolism*

Of course any discussion of a powerful theme like 'living water' seems to call for a fundamental definition of the very idea of symbolism. But the concept is so far-reaching that it would be foolhardy to attempt it in so small a space.[4] Instead I am grateful to Sandra M. Schneiders for a wholly apposite definition of the biblical symbol as 'a sensible reality which renders present to and involves a person subjectively in a transforming experience of transcendent mystery'.[5]

A symbol, then, is intended to express a transcendental reality that is not otherwise accessible. Admittedly, several aspects of this definition ought to be teased out more exhaustively. Here I shall merely stress the fact that a symbol is neither pure word play, as it were, nor a communication of objective data, but a summons to the interpreting subject to make a personal commitment to constructing a meaning not available in advance. By launching the act of interpretation,[6] the symbol transposes the encounter with transcendent reality in an experience that necessarily transforms the experiential subject. The significance of the symbol is never exhausted, and it will never proffer a unique, universally valid interpretation of symbolic reality. Each interpreter invests the symbol with his own experience. For instance, an African woman who has to spend part of her day fetching water to ensure her family's survival, a fisherman from Japan and a citizen of Paris cannot inform and decypher Johannine symbolism in exactly the same way.

Finally, the scope of the symbol is conditioned to a considerable extent by the natural properties of the symbolizing element or symbolizer. In the case of water, the symbolic activity will play on a few universally-recognized properties of physical water: it fertilizes, it springs up and maintains life, but it can also cause death; it slakes thirst; it dissolves, washes and purifies; it flows, spills over, seeps wherever there is no barrier, and fills empty spaces. Then these characteristics will be modulated depending on the constraints applied to the water as it flows: pent-up water (sea, lake, well, swimming pool), semi-free water (river, torrent), and free water spouting or falling (spring, fountain, rain).[7]

III The symbolic water of the fourth gospel

The term *hydôr*, 'water', appears 20 times in the fourth gospel, but does not always take on a symbolic dimension. In almost half the cases, it is its natural property of purification is evoked: the baptism by water of the Baptist (1.26, 31, 33; 3.23), water from jars for Jewish ablutions (2.7, 9; 4.46), and water to wash the disciples' feet (13.5). The word certainly acquires a symbolic charge when the suggested power of water imposes itself before its physical properties: the living water given and promised by Jesus (4.10, 11, 14; 7.38), the water that came from the pierced side of the crucified Christ (19.34), and of course the water, which, by virtue of the Spirit, brings about one's rebirth from on high (3.5).

It is important to note that the first references to water in John's gospel all seem to suggest a certain form of overflowing associated with the person of Jesus. In the first chapter, the *baptism of water* dispersed by John is linked to the revelation of Jesus, who *will baptize in the Holy Spirit*. It is difficult, at this stage in the narrative, to interpret the meaning of this baptism other than in association with the Old Testament promises that God would renew the Covenant and pour out his Spirit into people's hearts like pure water (cf. Is. 44.3; Ez. 36.25–7). Then, during the Wedding Feast of Cana, Jesus changes the water in six jars[8] into new wine, symbolizing eschatological salvation (cf. Amos 9.14; Joel 2.24–8). Even in John 3.3,5, rebirth from on high by the water of the Spirit explodes the traditional Jewish notion that only the blood descendants of Abraham would inherit the promises of the Covenant. This theme of overflowing certainly decides how the reader of the scene at the well is to approach it.

(a) *Living water in John 4.1–42*

Wishing to avoid a confrontation with the Pharisees of Jerusalem about his disciples' baptismal activities, Jesus wishes to return to his native Galilee by crossing Samaria. When he is close to Sychar (Shechem), he meets a Samaritan woman (a heretic in Jewish eyes), who has come to Jacob's Well in the middle of the day to draw water and take it back to her house. There could not have been a more striking contrast between this scene and Jesus' previous meeting, when Nicodemus, a *man*, and a *Pharisee* representing Jewish orthodoxy, came at *night* to enquire about

Jesus' teaching (cf. 3.1–2). In that case the *night* was the highly-symbolic image, whereas in the present instance the *well* performs that function.

Some important people in biblical history met their future wives at a well: Isaac (Gen. 24), Jacob (Gen. 29.1–30) and Moses (Ex. 2.15–22). The present episode displays the certain features common to these betrothal-type scenes,[9] but should possibly be read in conjunction with, and as a free reinterpretation of, Genesis 24 (*midrash*). This matrimonial coloration is reinforced by the insertion of the pericope in part of the gospel (2.1–4, 54), where Jesus' identity as messianic Spouse is heavily accentuated (cf. 2.1–12 and 3.27–9). There is an undeniably nuptial undertone to the meeting between Jesus and the woman of Samaria.

When Jesus sees the woman coming to draw water, he asks her for a drink. But the woman resists. She is probably offended by a stranger addressing her, but truly astonished that a Jew should think nothing of the impurity he would suffer from contact with a heretic's jar.[10] The first point of interest is that the water, even from a well inherited from ancestors, is shared over and above religious, ethnic and geopolitical barriers.

The woman's resistance is an exception to a script of the betrothal-scene variety,[11] for it might have brought the meeting to an end. But Jesus persists with a quite surprising change of perspective: '"If you knew what God can give," Jesus replied, "and if you knew who it is that said to you, 'Give me a drink', I think you would have asked him, and he would have given you living water!" (4.10 [Phillips]). Surely the water from the well is merely Jesus' pretext to direct the woman's attention to himself and to the living water that he alone can give? Since the only nourishment that Jesus accepts is to fulfil the mission that his Father gave him (cf. 4.31–8), the water from the well probably wouldn't quench his thirst[12] anyway. Another point of interest is the paradox that Jesus could satisfy his own thirst by giving living water to a woman and to the Samaritans.

Once again, the woman does not answer Jesus' proposal immediately. The well is deep and Jesus doesn't even have a bucket: '…where can you get your living water? Are you a greater man than our ancestor, Jacob?', she replies (4,11–12). Clearly, living water hasn't the same meaning for the two speakers. The woman, under the impetus of a real physical thirst that makes her go out in the heat of the day to draw water needed for her survival, thinks of living water as essentially a free water, springing out and much better than the water trapped in the well. She associates it with an inexhaustible spring that would not call for all this effort. She must be aware of the religious traditions of her ancestors, and especially the one which said that water from the well sprang forth miraculously before the patriarchs, a miracle that became even more striking in Jacob's case, because then the water had gushed out for 20 years without interruption.[13] But surely an invocation of ancestral tradition introduces thirst of another order: a thirst for knowledge, a spiritual thirst for salvation, if you know that the well Jacob gave his descendants was only an image of that other Well of mythic status: the well that never ceased to provide spiritual refreshment to refresh the people in the desert: in other words, the Torah, the source of Wisdom.[14]

Jesus sees the change and goes further: "'Everyone who drinks this water will be thirsty again. But whoever drinks the water I will give him will never be thirsty again. For my water will become a spring in the man himself, welling up into eternal life' (4.13–14). Ready for anything rather than the daily grind of fetching water just to live, the woman seizes the opportunity: "'Sir, give me this water, so that I may stop being thirsty...'" (4.15).

Her understanding of the situation is developing. Now she senses the possibility of a miracle, for she comes here to draw water every day and is well aware that water from the well does not quench thirst permanently. Yet she can only draw on her own experience in an attempt to determine the meaning of living water. She is impelled by a constant, intense human thirst. Jacob's water, even if it flows spontaneously, can only relieve this thirst momentarily. But what if Jesus is really greater than Jacob, and his living water can satisfy her thirst for ever?

Jesus' word evokes something other than the material water in the well. The call of Wisdom is recognizable now: 'Come to me, you who desire me...those who drink of me will thirst for more' (Sir. 24.19–21). In barely veiled words, the thirst contemplated by Jesus and the Samaritan woman is a spiritual thirst that the well inherited from the patriarchs, a source of Wisdom and knowledge of God, relieves but never fully satisfies. By asking for the living water, the woman is also aspiring to quench her thirst for salvation, while remaining within her own tradition. The third point of interest is that, in ancestral tradition, the living water is the Law, which dispenses Wisdom and knowledge of God. This living water is to salvation what natural water is to life.

Most commentators have noted the change of perspective during the discussion. First of all there is a water which Jesus could give the woman straightaway (v. 10). Then there is the water which he will give her in an indeterminate future, and which will become an inward source of everlasting life in whomsoever drinks it (v. 14). Taking this living water might well prove to be a protracted process leading to the *eschaton*, and one suspended between 'now' and 'not yet'.

The first step is taken 'here and now'. Henceforth assuming his role as giver of living water, Jesus responds to the woman's request. The conversation about husbands (John 4.16–18) does not carry the moralizing weight several commentators would ascribe to it. Admittedly we cannot elide a reference to Jesus' clairvoyant insight into the woman's personal love life, without which the recognition of Jesus as a prophet (4.19) would no longer have a narrative base, and there would be no basis for the testimony that Jesus 'told me everything I've ever done' (4.39).

But our female character would also seem to have a representative value for all her Samaritan co-religionists,[15] which suggests a second level of interpretation for the woman's love life. Perhaps the Greek word meaning 'husband' (*anēr*) conceals the Semitic term *ba'al*, that could refer to a divinity or to a husband. Since the Bible freely evokes adultery to condemn the people's idolatry and lack of religious faith, Jesus might also be referring to the pagan cults which the deportees from five Babylonian towns introduced into Samaria,[16] leading moreover to a syncretic deformation of the cult of Yahweh. Characterized by the same imperfection as the purifying water of the six jars at the wedding feast in Cana, the six Samaritan cults should be replaced by the perfect and definitive worship of the seventh husband/*ba'al*, God the Father, who must be adored in Spirit and in truth (cf. John 4.19–26).[17] Providing a wholly appropriate conclusion to the intertext of Genesis 24, Jesus, like the servant Eliezer, is preparing to conclude a Covenant, this time between the Samaritan people and the perfect God, the real eschatological Husband.

Undoubtedly the water offered to the Samaritans is the revelation of the Father, the bestowal of the truth that comes in the very person of Jesus (cf. 1.17).

(b) The living water is the Spirit (John 7.37–9)

How, then, are we to accommodate the interpretation given in Chapter 7, once Jesus has invited believers to come to him and drink, in accordance with Scripture: 'The man who believes in me, as the scripture said, will have rivers of living water flowing from his inmost heart' (7.37–8). Now the narrator states unequivocally: 'Here he was speaking about the Spirit which those who believe in him would receive. The Spirit has not yet been given because Jesus had not yet been glorified' (7.39). This passage obviously takes up the future prospect opened up in 4.14.

It is crucial to understand that John sees Jesus – Jesus as the person he is – as the fundamental symbol of God himself,[18] on which all the other theological symbols of this gospel depend. But, as I have emphasized, that which is symbolized could never dispense with that which signifies it corporeally and perceptibly. What will happen when Jesus leaves? One symbolizing element, or 'symbolizer', replaces another. The precise intention of Jesus' farewell speech (cf. 13–17) is to explain that he will be present in a different way after his glorification. He will pour the living water of the Spirit of truth onto his followers (cf. 19.34), and will bestow the indwelling power of his Word on the believer's heart.[19] This is the everlasting source of living water which springs from believers' innermost selves, and never ceases to satisfy their thirst for eternal life. The Samaritan woman would never need to return to the well to draw this water unceasingly.

IV Conclusion

How are we to treat this very unusual symbolic use of the living-water metaphor today? We do not have to adopt the sacramental interpretation, current in the Church from the second century, especially since it does not seem to apply to the original construction of the narrative. On the first level of symbolization, Word and Spirit quite certainly denote living water. But their relevance with regard to the natural properties of water is due to their capacity to convey knowledge of the Father, the unique source of true and definitive Life. The entire symbolic potential of water is deployed here. The living water bestows everlasting life by assuaging the creature's burning thirst for its Creator, and by penetrating to every part of a human being in order to endow it with the presence of the Son who cries: '*Abba*, Father!'. This thirst is experienced in Africa as in America. Everywhere on the blue planet, they call on the Son, saying: 'Give us this water so that we will never be thirsty again!'.

Translated by Felicity Leng

Notes

1. This episode in John 4 has always aroused the interest of commentators. There have been some outstanding feminist and post-colonial readings of the passage in recent years, directed mainly to the figure of the woman. Unfortunately they are beyond the scope of this article. But you should consult the article by Surekha Nelavala, 'Jesus asks the Samaritan woman for a drink: a Dalit-Feminist reading of John 4', *Lectio Difficilior 1* (2007), pp. 1–25 (http://www.lectio.unibe.ch), and Anne Béatrice Fayé's contribution to this issue of *Concilium*.
2. Literally, 'he has told (it)', from the Greek verb *exēgeomai*. The passage uses the *narrative* form to describe the revelation of the Father through the Son. The Father makes himself known through the life of his incarnate Son, then in the resulting gospel narrative.
3. Cf. 1 John 2.19. See J. L. Martyn, *History and Theology in the Fourth Gospel*, Nashville, ²1979; R. E. Brown, *The Community of the Beloved Disciple*, New York, 1979.
4. The now classic work by Gilbert Durand, *L'imagination symbolique*, Paris, ²1968, is still very useful; see also the semi-encyclopaedic work of Marc Girard, *Les symboles dans la Bible: essai de théologie biblique enracinée dans l'expérience humaine universelle*, Montreal & Paris, 1991.
5. Sandra M. Schneiders, *Written That You May Believe. Encountering Jesus in the Fourth Gospel*, New York, ²2003, p. 66.
6. Its etymology (from the Greek *sumballō*, literally 'to put together' or 'join') shows that the symbolic act is always one of joining two separate parts: as here, where the two elements are the corporeal or appreciable signifier, shown in the text, and the transcendent signified, that has to be reconstructed. Necessarily, then, a symbol requires 'interpretation'.
7. Cf. Marc Girard, *Les symboles...*, *op. cit.*, pp. 234–5.
8. The numerical symbol of imperfection (6=7–1): even when completely full, the six jars called for by the Jewish purification system cannot satisfy the needs of the wedding feast (that is: cannot bring about the salvation of the messianic age).
9. Cf. Robert Alter, *The Art of Biblical Narrative*, New York, ²2011, pp. 60–1.
10. After the woman's reply, the narrator loses no time in explaining that the Jews, who considered the Samaritans to be heretics, generally refused all contact with them, out of fear of exposure to ritual impurity. This was certainly not the case in John's community, which consisted partly of believers of Samaritan origin.
11. See J. E. Botha, 'Reader "Entrapment" a Literary Device in John 4.1–42', *Neotestamentica* 24 (1990), pp. 37–47.
12. In John 19.28 Jesus' thirst is explicitly interpreted as associated with the accomplishment of his mission.
13. Cf. Targum Neofiti and the Targums (or interpretative translations) of Jerusalem in Genesis 28.10 and 29.10.
14. There is no proof of the existence of an actual Jacob's Well in the Old Testament, or elsewhere in Jewish tradition. For the myth of the spiritual well, see especially the work of Annie Jaubert, and primarily 'La symbolique du Puits de Jacob. Jn. 4.12', in: *L'Homme devant Dieu*, vol. I, Paris, 1963, pp. 63–73; and 'Symbolique de l'eau et connaissance de Dieu', *Foi et Vie* 64 (1965), pp. 455–63. In wisdom literature, the living water refers to streams of wisdom, and instruction is to be drawn from the law

(cf. Prov. 13.14; 16.22; 18.4; Sir. 24.30ff); the lovers of wisdom conform to the Law of Moses (Sir. 24.23).
15. See Raymond F. Collins, 'The Representative Figures in the Fourth Gospel', *Downside Review* 94 (1976), pp. 26–46, 118–32.
16. Although the text of 2 Kings 17.24–41 cites seven pagan divinities, it seems that no such fine distinction was made in New Testament times, and five idolatrous sects are involved (cf. Flavius Joseph, *Ant.* 9.14.3., par. 288).
17. For this development, see Marc Girard, 'Jésus en Samarie (Jean 4,1–42). Analyse des structures stylistiques et du processus de symbolisation', *Église et Théologie* 17 (1986), pp. 301–6.
18. Cf. Sanda M. Schneiders, *Written...*, *op. cit.*, pp. 71–2.
19. Cf. Ignace de Le Potterie, 'Jésus et les Samaritains, Jn. 4.5–42', *Assemblée du Seigneur* 16 (1971), pp. 34–49.

African Women and Water

ANNE-BEATRICE FAYE CIC

I Introduction

Water problems are not the same throughout Africa. It is plentiful in certain areas because it rains a lot there. But finding enough water to satisfy a family's needs in semi-desert regions is a nightmare. Populations often depend on resources that vary according to season and rainfall. This article is mainly concerned with the Sahel (a desert belt that extends across several countries),[1] where, more than elsewhere, access to water is a constant preoccupation in women's everyday lives.

'Drinking, eating, making sure of a home, getting clothes, washing, doing the laundry, producing things, building, moving around, caring for yourselves, and so on, are demands of day-to-day living for which water is indispensable'.[2] You don't realize its quantitative or qualitative value until you're without it. Then, in the Sahel especially, the lack of access to drinking water is one of the basic causes of disease and death. Women are primarily responsible for the use and management of water and are constantly alive to the importance of domestic cleanliness and health. In Sahelian cultures, where the physical, anthropological, cultural and spiritual dimensions of water are closely linked, women are intimately concerned with every aspect of this precious liquid.

Water is very important culturally. Its use and significance run through the values, images and social organization of African society. In a study of the bases of African artistic creativity, Iba Ndiaye Diadji even evokes the essentially 'aquatic nature'[3] of being African. Water is a symbol of life, hospitality and purification. It is indispensable for invoking, praying, exorcism, reconciliation, expiation and communication. There are those who speak of the 'spirit of water', as if it were a living being whom you can talk to. Wise men say that 'there is more in water than crocodiles'. The river is full of spirits whom you can address. It is like a member of the family. You talk to it and persuade it to do this or that. In one story[4], for example, the Congolese writer Victor Nimy tells of a mother's intense love for her two children, who were carried away by the river, and how she forces it to give them back to her. The mother speaks so much to the river and weeps so movingly on its banks that eventually it surrenders them to her. Birago Diop, a Senegalese poet well-known in Africa, says: 'The dead never go away/...They are in the flowing water. / They are in the sleeping water. / No, the dead are not dead. / You must listen more to things than to people./ Yes, you must listen to the voice of the water.'[5]

Who is more liable to hear the water speak than an African woman? In this article I try to describe the association between African women and water as shown in narratives, rules of life, and hard work, and then give a short account of the appeals of John Paul II and international organizations for due resolution of the vast problem of the water shortage in Africa. I close this contribution with some remarks on what is probably the biblical story related to this topic that is most richly and subtly appropriate to it: the meeting between Jesus and the Samaritan woman at the well of Sychar (Shechem), and what they say to each other about water (John 4).

I   Woman and water, sources of life

In Africa a large number of myths are linked to water.[6] A few from the countries of the Sahel belt, and from Mali in particular, are pertinent to our theme. The creation story is a primordial type of myth. In the case of the Bambaras from Mali, for example, the myth tells us that the creation of the world took place when Pemba, a heavy mass, fell in a whirlwind, and gave birth to the earth. At the same time, a fragment of spirit rose up, and Faro used it to construct the sky. Then Faro fell to earth in the form of water, and endowed it with life, especially aquatic animals. Faro also plays a fascinating part in the film *Faro, Goddess of the Waters*, by the Malian director Salif Traoré.[7] Another myth holds that the Dogon people of Mali are very conscious of the links which unite them to the four elements: the water they drink, the air they breathe, the sun that heats them and the food they ingest. In their cosmography, water is a seed of divine origin and green in colour. It impregnates the earth to produce exceptional green twins that are half-men, and half-snakes. The union of two waters in the guise of seeds also provided life for the human race. A Dogon wise man tells of the belief that, when God, Nommo, 'mated with

Earth, he deposited his seed, which consists of water, by spreading it. This vital universal force took the form of humidity impregnating every shape in the physical world'. Furthermore, 'Women', says the Dogon sage, 'are our aqueducts. Without them, water would never come to the village'. Logically, therefore, there is a connection between the words 'water' and 'woman'. On the high plains of Bandiagra, in Mali, the entire body of myths, beliefs and perceptions of the sacred, of social behaviour and the division of labour, entrusts women with the duty of ensuring that the whole community has water, which is ultimately life.[8]

The female cares for water as the seed and origin of life, and there are several associated rites for the birth of a child. For instance, the new-born infant is welcomed with water and the word: 'One of the women who was present at the birth takes water in her mouth and sprinkles her spittle lightly on the child. The cold water makes the newcomer to earth cry out. It has received the word formally'.[9] Spitting on someone with ordinary water purifies the recipient, but spitting with saliva is a blessing in the name of the ancestors. This rite highlights the importance of the water-woman union in the development of speech. It is a matter of symbolically returning the child to the element of water (the ecosystem) which it has just left, and which is life itself, but this time with something additional, which is language. The child finds its place in the new milieu (ecosystem). In the case of the Sérers of Senegal, the woman gives the baby its first bath. A fragment of Bân (a very hard wood, signifying a firm and solid life), is placed in the bath water, together with a piece of iron (a sign of resistance, of sacred power from the world above) and a twig of Sin (a plant well-known for its reproductive strength, symbolizing the active diffusion of beliefs and a sign of an effective personality).

A conception of the world in which everything finds its origin lies behind all these myths, beliefs and practices. Water influences human life and marks every moment of every day that passes. It plays a role in an immense number of actions and gestures that punctuate everyday existence.

II How to behave

Among the rules of conduct in Africa, which are exercised by women, the offering of water to welcome someone is a key element in the culture of the continent. The water that a woman gives you the moment you cross the threshold of her home, whether you are thirsty or not, expresses the wish that the power of water will reduce your suffering or strengthen your serenity. The water that a woman pours before or behind people on their arrival and departure is always accompanied by a prayer that peace and happiness should guide their footsteps. Joseph Ki-Zerbo, a well-known writer and politician in Burkina Faso, describes a traveller's experience: 'On many occasions when my vehicle broke down in the bush, a young girl would approach me and offer me water. Nobody had asked for this water, but it is a right for those who come from elsewhere'.[10] In African culture, water is like air: a common asset, a right, and not some kind of commodity for sale.

In everyday life, the windows of houses, galleries, artists' studios, the displays in the markets, the shop doors run by Africans, are doused with water in the very early morning. Car wheels are often sprayed with water, daily, at the garage exit. On her wedding day, a daughter is blessed with water in which plants symbolizing gentleness, happiness and marital harmony have been dipped. The water chases away evil forces and bad spirits, and eliminates stains.

There is also the traditional gesture of pouring a little water on the ground before you drink, because the ground is seen as an entity which must be served first. If hot water is inadvertently poured onto the earth, cold water is fetched immediately to pour on the same spot, in order to appease the ancestors. It is not rare to see a woman pour some water on the footsteps of her son, a university professor, when he leaves for, or comes back from, Europe. He keeps a little bottle of water in his knapsack to hold any kind words said.

These different practices mean that water wards off evil and invokes peace, success and prosperity for everyone. It renews relations with the world of the ancestors. Whether it comes from a tap in the hotel or is bottled spring water bought from a supermarket, whether it is from a well or a river, water is and always remains a deep symbol in the mind and practice of many Africans.

IV The hard labour of Sahelian women

For women living on the edge of the desert, water has rich and vital implications, but obtaining it every day causes them great suffering. In the Sahel, the devastation brought about by the lack of water is glaringly obvious. The wells are contaminated and running water is rare. Its use for irrigation and industry leaves entire populations without it.[11] The work of Sahelian women and daughters very often revolves around the arduous and difficult transport of water, the source of life. Most of them have to cover miles to get water from the nearest well or river.

Very early in the morning, women and daughters go mainly to wells to draw water. The pitiful spectacle of hundreds of women and children carrying water cans and basins, in perpetual quest for water, is familiar in this region. Every day they cover an average of six kilometres on foot to fetch a few litres of water. The problem of access to water often means that the youngest women have to abandon school, which perpetuates inequality between the sexes.[2] In fact, the situation of women is clearly better in regions where a clean water supply and sanitation are provided. They have more time to concentrate on the health of the family, to develop income-generating activities, and, in the case of daughters, to go to school and live out their adolescence. But the challenge of ensuring a water supply and access to water is far-reaching.

V   Water, an inalienable right

The Catholic Church has issued many important messages on sharing water.[13] Its essential character as a gift from God requires it to be shared equally. The Church's social doctrine defines access to water as a 'universal and inalienable right...water by its nature cannot be treated as a simple commodity among many others and its use should be rational and shared. The right to water, like all human rights, is based on human dignity and not on purely quantitative assessments, which treat water as no more than an economic asset. Life is under threat without water'.[14] On 10 May 1980, when the countries of the Sahel seemed to be wholly devastated by the rigours of an implacable drought, a voice spoke out to awaken the conscience of a world that was powerless and indifferent in the face of this distressing experience. When Pope John Paul II kissed the ground for the first time in the Sahel, he was shocked by the ecological desolation which he encountered in the real world behind the television images. He launched an historic appeal from Ouagadougou in these terms: 'I am launching an appeal. I, John Paul II, Bishop of Rome and Successor of Peter, raise my voice in supplication, because I do not wish to keep silence when my brothers and sisters are threatened. Here I speak for those who have no voice, for the innocent who died because they lacked bread and water, for fathers and mothers who watched uncomprehendingly as their children died, or still see them display the after-effects of the hunger they have endured. I speak for generations to come who should no longer have to live with this terrible threat weighing on their lives'.[15] His voice echoed and re-echoed and started a chain of solidarity resulting in the creation of the John Paul II Foundation for the Sahel.[16] International organizations have also made many efforts to manage, economize on, clean water and respond to it as a universal challenge.[17] Some have established sanitation and potable water-supply systems[18], in order to increase the quality of life, mainly of the women of the Sahel. Since all the problems linked to water are interdependent, they have to be tackled in conjunction. Kofi Annan, former UN Secretary General, explained in this respect: 'We can only come to terms with AIDS, tuberculosis, malaria and other infectious diseases that afflict the developing world when we have won the battle for clean drinking water and primary health care'.[19] The lack of access to water affecting so many people represents an opportunity to live in solidarity not only nationally but internationally.

VI Water as a spiritual dimension; the well as a theological location for us now

In the foregoing I recalled the hard labour of Sahelian women with regard to water, water as an inalienable universal right, the inequality of the sexes due to the division of labour, and some symbolic meanings of water. Now I shall try to probe the cultural and religious implications of water, and in particular the deep and indissoluble relation between water, women and life. These two viewpoints help us to understand one of the most instructive episodes in the Bible in connection with the present topic: Jesus' meeting with the Samaritan woman at Jacob's Well (John 4).[20]

Jesus rested at the edge of the well. He was tired and thirsty after his journey, and asked for a drink. He wanted to quench his thirst, and thereby satisfy a natural need. This image of Jesus as an ordinary man reveals his humanity and poverty, and merges with that of Sahelian women in our own times, running with sweat, going yet again to join the others at the well and bearing jerry cans on their heads. The Samaritan woman also reflects the real lives of Sahelian women, for she has come to fetch the essential water needed by her household, and that is the hard daily grind of all those deprived of water. Jacob's Well is associated with at least two important stories in the Old Testament. It was close to Sychar (Shechem), that Dinah, the daughter of Jacob, was raped by the son of the prince of the region, outside the city (Gen. 34). Accordingly, the name Jacob and the place recall all the risks of aggression and rape in unsafe areas when women go to fetch water. On the other hand, it was at the well that the patriarch Jacob met his future wife, Rachel (Gen. 29.1–12), for a well is a place of meeting and exchange.[21]

Jesus and the Samaritan woman engage in a conversation based on the daily and natural need for water (people are thirsty and people have to drink), which progresses to a spiritual level: 'Jesus said to her: "Everyone who drinks this water will be thirsty again. But whoever drinks the water I will give him will never be thirsty again. For my gift will become a spring in the man himself, welling up into eternal life". The woman said: "Sir, give me this water, so that I may stop being thirsty—and not have to come here to draw water any more!"' (John 4.13–15).

Jesus passes from the water from Jacob's Well to the water that gives spiritual life. The Samaritan woman opens her mind and spirit to the truth of this stranger who shows himself to be the Messiah, the only source that can satisfy her thirst: 'Ho, everyone who thirsts, come to the waters…' (Is. 55.1). 'With joy you will draw water from the wells of salvation' (Is. 12.3). 'So the woman left her water-pot behind and went into the town and began to say to the people: "Come out and see the man who told me everything I've ever done! Can this be 'Christ'?"' (John 4.28–9).

The glazed jug at the side of the well was designed to draw water and transport it to the village. By abandoning it, the Samaritan lets go of her daily preoccupations. By receiving the living water, she becomes a witness to the Gospel. She will take what she has learned to the village, no longer carrying it in a jug but in her heart, which enthuses over her discovery of the 'Messiah', the Christ. John Paul II referred to this aspect of the story of the Samaritan woman in his homily in Ouagadougou: 'We are all like this Samaritan woman. We all thirst for the truth that comes from God. We all thirst for the truth about ourselves, about the meaning of our lives, about what we can and should do, from now on, wherever we are, to respond to what God expects of each one of us, to make us really part of his family and live as children of God'.[22]

The personal meeting with Jesus led the Samaritan woman to discover a new horizon of spirituality and a new image of God, giver of life. She will find the fullness of life she yearns for in her meeting with the living God bestowed on her in the person of Jesus Christ: 'Happy are those who do not follow the path of the wicked...They are like trees planted by streams of water, which yield their fruit in its season, and their leaves do not wither. In all that they do they prosper' (cf. Ps. 1).

VII   Conclusion

The division between North and South, and between East and West, is mainly attributable to the fact that very rich countries are oblivious to these primary experiences of thirst and the labour needed to find water. Sahelians cannot ignore them. Every day, women especially have to do demanding work to procure water. Important narratives and rites make use of water in ways that that are still very significant in the lives of the inhabitants of the water-poor Sahel belt. In that region defending the right to water means defending the right to life. Promising an end to thirst is the ultimate promise, and this spiritual metaphor could not be more relevant (cf. John 4.13): 'Everyone who drinks this water will be thirsty again. But whoever drinks the water I will give him will never be thirsty again'.

The symbolic link between women and water in the context of the Sahel experience might well inspire us to change the ways in which we manage water and live out our interpersonal relationships. It could also make us more supportive of the most under-privileged on this earth. We might also find that we are vouchsafed experiences of deprivation and longing that bring us closer to God. The most human choices are open to us only if we start from the most vulnerable circumstances. In this sense, water is indeed an essential topic for theology in general, and one with even greater ramifications in African theology.

Translated by Felicity Leng

Notes

1. The Sahel covers a vast area of Africa extending from Senegal to Sudan. The Sahel (or Sahelian) belt runs across numerous African countries (Senegal, Mauritania, Mali, Algeria, Burkina Faso, Niger, Nigeria, Chad, Sudan, Cape Verde) and certain authorities would include Ethiopia, Eritrea, Djibouti and Somalia. Its location on the periphery of the desert subjects the Sahel to a fluctuating climate and intermittent drought. Rainfall is rare and water is so precious that it has to be managed carefully.
2. Zakari Bouraima, *Cours d'anthropologie d'eau* (Institut international d'ingénierie de l'eau et de l'environnement [International institute of water and environmental 82/collect/eauetass/index/assoc/HASHb5d6.dir/doc.pdf)
3. Iba Ndiaye Diadji, 'De l'eau- vie à l'eau-mort ou les fondements de la création artistique africaine d'hier à demain', http://www.olats.org/africa/projets/gpEau/genie/contrib/contrib_diadji.shtml.
4. Kalla Victor Nimy, *La noyée. Conte beembé du Congo*, Paris, 2002.
5. Birago Diop, *Leurres et lueurs*, n.p., 1960, p. 64.
6. Mohamed Larbi Bouguera, *Symbolique et culture de l'eau* (Les rapports de l'Institut Véolia environnement), Paris, n.d. ,pp.16–19;http://www.institut.veolia.org/fr/ressources/cahiers/CCA5GJz4FUfi9Ohi75PVst3j.pdf.
7. Cf. http://www.ferdyonfilms.com/2007/faro-goddess-of-the-waters-2007/221/.
8. Cf. Domenico Luciani, 'Des mythes à la réalité', in: *Manière de voir*, No. 65 (*La ruée vers l'eau*), September–October 2002, pp. 24–7, cited by L. M. Bouguerra, *Symbolique...*, *op. cit.*, p. 18.
9. Louis-Vincent Thomas & René Luneau, *La terre africaine et ses religions. Traditions and changes*, Paris, 1980, pp. 117–18.
10. Cf. UN Report on the *Development of Water in the World*, http://unesdoc.unesco.org/images/0021/002154/215491f.pdf.
11. See especially the Contribution of the Holy See at the VI World Water Forum (Marseilles, France, March 2012): *Water, an essential element for life. To inaugurate efficient solutions* (Vatican Council: Justice and Peace); http://www.vatican.va/roman_curia/pontifical_councils/justpeace/documents/rc_pc_justpeace_doc_20120312_france-water_fr.html .Cf. also the contributions of the Pontifical Justice and Peace Council for 2009 and 2006.
12. Pontifical Justice and Peace Council (ed.), *Compendium of the Social Doctrine of the Church*, Nos 481–5. http://www.vatican.va/roman_curia/pontifical_councils/justpeace/documents/rc_pc_justpeace_doc_20060526_compendio-dott-soc_fr.html; cf. also Benedict XVI, *Caritas in veritate*, par. 27. http://www.vatican.va/holy_father/benedict_xvi/encyclicals/documents/hf_ben-xvi_enc_20090629_caritas-in-veritate_fr.html.
13. John Paul II, Homily of 10 May 1980 at Ouagadougou. http://www.vatican.va/holy_father/john_paul_ii/homilies/1980/documents/hf_jp-ii_hom_19800510_ouagadougou-africa_fr.html.
14. http://www.fondationjeanpaul2.org.
15. Cf. *The African Vision of Water*, presented at the second World Water Forum, held at The Hague in 2000 when a special African water facility fund was set up to be administered by the African Development Bank (BAD).
16. SOS SAHEL conducts projects for water access in various countries. See http://www.sossahel.org/, Water and Sanitation Projects in Burkina Faso, Rharous Mali, Dara in Mauritania and Kati in Mali. The progress achieved in sub-Saharan

Africa is impressive, and coverage has increased from 49 per cent in 1990 to 58 per cent in 2002. But even at this rate it will not be possible to reach the objective of the UN Millennium Declaration for development set for 2015. Cf. *Water and culture. International decade of freshwater 2005–2015. Third World Forum of Water*, 22. 2003; see http://www.who.int/water_sanitation_health/Water&cultureFrench.pdf.

17. Kofi Annan, *Celebrating Water for Life. The International Decade for Action 2005–2015* (cf.http://www.who.int/water_sanitation_health/2005advocguide/fr/index.html.
18. This text is widely discussed in English-speaking African theology. I recommend Sylvain Vianney Bamana, 'A Biblical and African reading of the meeting between Jesus and the Samaritan woman (John 4.5–26)', *Mundo Marianista* 3 (2005), pp. 256–72; cf. http://www.mundomarianista.org/wp-content/uploads/vol3-fas2-La-escritura-en-nuestra-vida-S-Bamana-SM-fr.pdf.
19. S. V. Bamana, *op. cit.*, p. 264.
20. Jean Paul II, Homily of 10 May 1980 at Ouagadougou.
21. S. V. Bamana, *op. cit.*, p. 264.
22. Jean Paul II, Homily of 10 May 1980 at Ouagadougou.

Feminine Waterscapes
Water as a Gendered Subject

KUNTALA LAHIRI-DUTT

Introduction

On average our bodies consist of 60 per cent water by weight (somewhat higher for men and lower for women). Nothing is more fundamental to life than water, and human beings cannot survive for more than a few days without it. The importance of water's physical presence in human lives is shown by its privileged place in the human imagination and cosmologies. Wagner[1] points out that water has a *social* life (a term used broadly to encompass all domains of human relationships, including the political, economic, and spiritual), for, although it circulates among all life forms and between animate and inanimate worlds, the human social connections which water brings into play constitute one sub-set of a broader set of ecological relations.

This concept of water is opposed to D. Haraway's[2] view that 'nature cannot pre-exist its construction', or to the Marxist idea of the appropriation and transformation of nature as social production. More recent views of nature have contested both extremes. For example, Linton's presentation of 'water is what we make of it',[3] in response to the query 'what is water', resonates with this notion. If, as Naguib suggests, '...water makes and unmakes human life and bonds, sensory experiences and relationships with cosmological forces', then, logically, it would be closely connected to gender relations that are part of and shaped by social factors.[4] There are, indeed, similarities between water and gender. For instance, water assumes the shape of the container which it fills, and gender, too, is 'never fixed, always fluid' (J. Butler). Metaphorically and representationally, water and gender are everywhere around us in our everyday lives. Water is 'what we make of it', and gender, too, is seen as a social construction. Water, like gender, can be perceived and presented differently in accordance with one's disciplinary training or preferences. The scientist sees water as a physical object and as an element that is only part of the physical environment, whereas the economist views it as a commodity, and the politician thinks of it as a national good to be planned and managed by the State.

The trans-disciplinary view of water also encourages gendered imaginations of this vital substance. Within global policy and activist domains, the gendering of waterscapes has involved disclosing women's and men's different uses of, needs for and interests in water, drawing upon gender inequalities in prioritizing women's and men's knowledge, highlighting different needs and concerns in managing water in various contexts, and reflecting on the distinct crises and contingencies that women and men in diverse societies have to face in their everyday lives.

The first part of this article describes the manifold relations between water and gender. In the second part, I shall show how water has been viewed as a gendered physical element in India. For this purpose I shall draw on two privileged sites,[5] and two sets of literature: the traditional Sanskrit texts that describe water holistically as part of nature, and popular, or folk, representations of rivers in India.

Part 1

I Re-conceptualizations of water

Of course, these images are embedded in radically different contexts. Accordingly, I heed Laurie L. Patton's observation[6] that 'to claim something about ecology is, in part, to claim a certain kind of unity: to invoke nature is to invoke primordial balance, holism, biological economy, understanding of interrelationships between things...to put it succinctly, cosmology is usually in the service of some form of ecology...Both ecologists and Indologists have resorted to ancient texts to describe Indian ideas about the cosmological workings of nature and to recover an understanding of balance and harmony within that world'. My interpretation draws upon recent work by Jane Bennett,[7] who queries the 'habit of parsing the world into dull matter (it, things) and vibrant life (us, beings)' to create what she describes as 'vibrant materiality,' in order to reinvigorate the belief in the spontaneity of nature.

Entering this domain of feminine waterscapes has proved rewarding. It has allowed us to understand how gender negotiates with an element of nature in different contexts and in accordance with various geographical scales, and encourages more intelligent and sustainable forms of engagement with the vibrant and lively gendered world of water. This article emphasizes not so much the active powers issuing from gendered waters as the gendered representations of waters. However, immense theoretical possibilities are offered by a revision and re-conceptualization of water as vital and living, compared with the current instrumental and functionalist interpretation. Its rehandling in this way may even lead to the emergence of more ecological and more materially sustainable modes of production and consumption of water.

II 'Fluid bonds'

Water, like gender, is known for its fluidity, for changing its shape and taking new forms. It plays a special role in social and cultural constructions of the environment, for water plays a vital part in 'conceptualizing universalist ideas of common humanity', and 'the essentiality of water also means that there is much common ground in interactions with it'.[9] The numerous worlds of water offer many paradoxes that are yet to be fully understood. Life begins and ends in water; all living things develop in an aqueous medium in their own genetically-defined ways, water heals and interacts with our bodies and, when life leaves a human body, water is sprinkled on those who are still alive. Water is a symbol which functions in terms not only of peace, life, and regeneration, but of femininity. The significance of water in human culture has often been expressed in spiritual, religious or social rituals, imbuing it and its users with meaning and value. According to Veronica Strang:[10] 'Water is always a metaphor of social, economic and political relationships: a barometer of the extent to which identity, power and resources are shared'.

Water is commonly seen only as a part of the physical environment, and is studied by tracking the pathways of the hydrological cycle and biological associations. However, much of what we make of water belongs to the domain of human culture; hence cultural and social norms are reflected in the ways in which water is used, perceived, governed and treated. Water is an integral part of our cultural landscape, and it is rooted in human history insofar as our history is connected to water. Waters is producer and product of the material culture through which a human agency operates. Engaging with water in the environment through sensory experiences and cognitive interpretations leads to the formation of cultural values and practices involving water.

III Gender and water: many connections

Gendered attributes and relations are highly contingent; they are always in a state of flux. I use 'gender' here to mean the roles and responsibilities of, and the social relationship between, women and men. Currently this relationship is unbalanced or asymmetrical, is based more on perceived social differences than on sex, anatomy or biology, and is founded on ideologies regarding the actors' roles, rights and values as workers, producers, owners, community members and citizens. Gender is not just a social construction, but a lived experience. Gender creates differences in the patterns of economic life histories for women and men dealing with water, and can lead to the adoption of different livelihood strategies. Economic differences among 'women' reflect inequalities in modes of production, class, race, location and ethnicity or caste. Gender is fundamentally relational and historically situated, and the whole range of hierarchical social relations in which women and men participate operates to construct the experience of gender. Even when using gender as a primary lens of observation, these other constructed hierarchies come into view, for gender is defined with, not apart from, race, class, and nationality. 'Women' do not constitute a unitary, homogeneous category, for they are located by multiple identities in different classes, ethnic or caste groupings and religions. Even within one country, it is difficult to generalize about the lived experiences of women. The importance of a gender view is evident when we consider the multitude of differences (of colour, caste, race, ethnicity, location and other power imbalances) that characterize women.

To make sense of water as a gendered substance inhabiting the cultural domain, we need to look closely and critically at the ways we live each part of our lives, for it is a gendered resource encoded with cultural, social, political, spiritual and environmental meanings. These in turn have a powerful effect on the uses of water, on the relationships between those who use it, and on those who supply it. Water takes on gendered understandings and meanings in a wider range of cultural contexts. Gender codes, themselves a changing feature, are inscribed on water in everyday lives. Through a watery lens, we encounter new realities and aesthetics of gender and place. Understanding these gendered relationships with water as much as with other elements of the environment unique to the place is a first step towards making gender visible in water issues.

Part 2

IV Water: a gendered physical element in India

Attitudes to water in the Upaniṣhads
Ancient Hindu texts are a good source of cosmological and ecological views that prevailed in India well before our contemporary ways of thought evolved. Laurie L. Patton notes[11] that: 'Both ecologists and Indologists have resorted to ancient texts to describe it in the ideas about the cosmological workings of nature and to recover an understanding of balance and harmony within that world…both appeal to a kind of romantic idea of nature in the abstract, which is only part of the picture suggested by the ancient Indian milieu itself.' The primordial balance, holism or oneness suggested by a popular conception of Hinduism as underlying the apparent diversity of the universe is a rather simplistic approach to natural elements.

The place of water within this complexity is perhaps best illustrated when set against the attitude towards its 'natural' counterpart, fire (*agni*). The term '*agni*' is used to denote both the element of fire and the personified god of fire; denoting both a natural element and a personable figure of the natural realm. *Varuna*, the god of the waters, or at least closely associated with them, is never identified with the waters themselves. Fire is readily associated with sacrifice by virtue of its capacity of consuming everything that comes into contact with it. Water, on the other hand, does not consume, and unlike oblational fire, 'carries life forward'. Heesterman[12] comments that one need only think of the frequent consecratory baths (consecration in the waters of the prospective soma sacrifice, or the consecratory showers undergone by the sacrifice) to be reminded of the important role of the aquatic element in ancient rituals. Mythological notions emphasize the intimate relationship of aquatic and igneous elements, albeit in an oppositional yet complementary association in which they are indispensable yet ambiguous. For example, fire can be generated and controlled by humans, whereas water cannot be controlled or fetishized in the same way as fire. Water appears in separate, manageable categories: as the primary aqueous element (*ap*, or the plural *apa*, meaning the waters), as rain (*varsha*), or as the oceans (*samudra*). *Ap* is the closest approximation to a general term for all these manifestations, yet is not an over-arching notion of water in the same way as *agni* is a term for fire.

Immersion in water as the obvious opposite of consumption by fire cannot be quite so easily balanced with the need for a reciprocal action. Water is threatening because it represents the limits of our ability to tame the substance into a reductive cosmology that can be neatly structured into a hierarchy of existence. Yet the very fact that water cannot be rehandled in that way makes it an almost irresistible metaphor for understanding the constructs and manipulations of the human world, especially in the appropriateness of the ocean as a representation of complete immersion in the infinite and in oneness. Therefore the image of water persists as a motif for many of the most important and powerful forces within ancient Hindu texts, almost in spite of its evident place within its overt cosmological framework. Water is the intermediary between the gaseous and the solid, being incorporated between *prana* (life) and *tejas* (heat), the 'other world' and 'this world', and the organic (often plants) and the inorganic (often the earth). Water is the essence or *rasa* of all beings in the earth, and the essence of all beings is the earth.

The conception of the waters as the primordial womb, the locus of cosmogonic processes, and the receptacle within which the cosmos rests is the key. It builds the context within which water is presented in its most gendered form and is intimately associated with the feminine. Within the womb, that is the river's bed, the flow of the water represents the surge of time itself.[13] Sacred rivers represent the ever-present stream of whom and what we essentially are: not a static being, but 'a dynamic ever-becoming flow of godlike radiance'.[14] According to Tambs-Lyche,[15] this worship of a natural element such as the river as feminine is a South Asian tradition, in contradistinction to the Christian imagery of rivers as masculine.[16] In the *Rigveda*: (Mandala/book 10; sukta/poem 75): 'this fierce river is going straight, her complexion is fair and bright, she is great, her swift-flowing waters are filling up everywhere. She is the fastest. She is like a horse. She is perfectly shaped as a swollen woman.

Sindhu is ever youthful and beautiful; she has an exquisite horse, a chariot, and beautiful clothes, has golden jewellery [in which] she has dressed up well'.

Nevertheless, throughout the Upanishads, and in Indian thought in general, various alternative formulations also associate the aquatic element with the masculine, although this tends to be when it is conflated with semen and with rain impregnating the earth. The water/ocean, however, is possibly more significant for the wider correspondence between water and the locus or receptacle than for that with the feminine as such. Water is more commonly perceived as a receptacle (as the womb, and so on) in relation to the feminine than water conceived of as an element pure and simple. The regenerative capacities of water in the annual rhythm of the cycle of nature are praised in the *Chāndogya Upaniṣhad* (5.10.1–6): 'Having become a thunder-cloud [the deceased villager] becomes a storm cloud; having become a storm cloud [the storm cloud] pours forth rain. They [then] arise as rice and barley, plants and trees, sesame and beans in this world, and it is truly most difficult to escape [the cycle], for [then in] semen issues from whomsoever eats the food [the rice, barley etc] and [the villager] comes into being [that is, experiences rebirth].' The femininity of water is intimately linked to this 'worldly' earthiness of human rebirth experienced by the villager and in everyday life.

Attitudes to rivers in folk life
Contemporary life also offers various social constructions of water. For instance, in deltaic Bengal,[17] a land formed by rivers, the boundaries between land and water interpenetrate and merge with the feminine identities of the rivers. Rivers are always present in the collective consciousness of Bengal. They are not only symbols but profoundly meaningful physical manifestations of concepts central to the cultural corpus of religious and communal lives. The river in the delta is seen as a potent symbol of feminine power inherent in nature; its waters of life symbolize fecundity and the cyclic movement of germination, and the growth and decay of life. This imagined river is not just a docile female, but possesses an inherent ferocity and brutality, and tremendously destructive powers. But she can also be benevolent, forgiving and giving. She offers sensory pleasures: '…the river bends down willingly as the mother bends down to breast-feed the son, and the young woman bends

down to embrace the young man.' This symbolic river is a duality, a combination of *shakti* (energy/power) and *prakriti* (nature), the two facets of femininity, yet also represents women as nature in its essentially uncultured, powerful and dangerous aspects.

This tendency might be said to express a contempt for, and fear of, women rooted in patriarchal Indian society established by Manu. The recurrent symbolism of seeding of the earth is not uncommon in Bengal folklore, and may have a somewhat sinister intent, for it makes a woman a commodity to be subjected to men. Yet the principle of power is expressed in the goddesses representing *shakti*, who come to the aid of humankind and the gods in periods of cosmic darkness by killing the demons who threaten the entire cosmic order. Similarly, rivers may be perceived as manifestations of divine feminine power, or *shakti*, since millions of people live along them and depend on them for their livelihood.

V Gendering water cultures

We have come a long way from ancient texts to contemporary folk life. Yet there is a continuity in the way in which the literate, scripture-based Sanskrit tradition of Vedic Hinduism has been carried forward by folk communities practising a kind of grassroots 'village Hinduism' offering a 'little tradition' of spiritual respect for the feminine aspects of the waters.[18] As F. Baartamans[19] remarks, 'No pure rational thought will reveal the waters. It is not meant to reveal these [waters],' because intellectualized rational thought overlooks the receptive consciousness of the sacred pervading the *āpah*, the waters, and entering into the entire life of a man, a woman, a child, an animal, a plant, a stone and the seasons, which all participate in the throbbing of the universe. As it removes dirt and filth, water also metabolizes waste matter, like a living organism.[20]

Furthermore, policy decisions on water, such as returning environmental flows to rivers, may reflect larger discourses, cultural values and norms within societies, which often include gendered constructs, for water itself possesses masculine or feminine characteristics. Attributes thought of as masculine and feminine affect aspects of our relationship with water. It is not too far-fetched to say that recognizing such deep cultural values implicit in decisions regarding water resource management may improve our understanding and future care of hydrological processes.

Looking at water through the lens of gender may also help us to contest the masculinist nature of the knowledge and understanding of water, and challenge the notions of gender-neutral scholarship on the subject. Analyzing gendered examples from ancient texts and their continuations in contemporary folk life can be illuminating. Water is not 'shapeless', as we are led to believe, but assumes multifarious cultural forms affecting human behaviour in respect of physical elements and their perception. Its applications reflect gendered values in every facet of our lives. This cultural realm comprises the whole spectrum of attitudes and values. The way in which human society looks at water has changed significantly over time, reflecting shifting values and creating new terrain for contestation. Examples of perceiving water as a feminine element are not difficult to find and prompt us to ask whether water is to women as land is to men.

The norms and laws governing how we deal with water that have evolved over the last 200 years or so embody masculinist values. These values include individual ownership, control through technology and the primacy of production as the best use for water. It is important to identify the close links with power relationships in society because masculinist controls over water destabilize women's perception and knowledge of water and the ways in which they engage with it.

On closer acquaintance, apparently gender-neutral norms and values are shown to be intertwined with deep-set cultural values – and always with gender concepts. A class-based analysis can also be used to assess the actual degree of divergence between women's and men's relations to the environment, and to identify constantly-changing compulsions and contradictions in women's own lives in quite different contexts and circumstances. This consideration of local, regional, national and international differences and distinctions also applies to the study and analysis of water, which is now a major theme and concern.

Notes

1. J. Wagner (ed.), *The Social Life of Water*, New York & Oxford, 2012, p. 3.
2. D. Haraway, 'The promises of monsters: A regenerative politics of inappropriate/d others', in: L. Grossberg, C. Nelson & P. A. Treichler (eds), *Cultural Studies*, New York, 1992, pp. 295–335, esp. p. 296.

3. J. Linton, *What is Water?: The History of a Modern Abstraction*, Vancouver, 2011, p. 2.
4. N. Naguib, in J. Wagner (ed.), *The Social Life of Water, op. cit.*
5. M. Asaduddin & M. Hasan have pointed out that the folk literature of Bengal reveals, perhaps better than any other form, the 'working of ideology in the lived experience of society'.
6. L. L. Patton, *Jewels of Authority: Women and Textual Tradition in Hindu India*, Oxford, 2002, pp. 39–40.
7. Jane Bennett, *Vibrant Matter: A Political Ecology of Things*, Durham & London, 2010, p. vii.
8. Cf. the title of my book: K. Lahiri-Dutt (ed.), *Fluid Bonds: Views on Gender and Water*, Kolkata, 2006.
9. V. Strang, *The Meaning of Water*, Oxford, 2004, p. 5.
10. *Ibid*, p. 21.
11. Laurie L. Patton, *Bringing the Gods to Mind: Mantra and Ritual in Early Indian Sacrifice*, Berkeley, CA, 2005. (N.B.: I wish to thank Professor McComas Taylor of the Australian National University and Andrew McGarrity of the University of Sydney for their kind assistance in interpreting the ancient Sanskrit texts which I have cited or drawn on for this essay).
12. J. C. Heesterman, *The Inner Conflict of Tradition: Essays in Indian Ritual, Kinship, and Society*, Chicago, 1985.
13. J. Swain, *Rivers of Time*, London, 1995.
14. W. T. S. Thackara, 'Sacred Rivers,' *Sunrise* October–November 2003.
15. H. Tambs-Lyche (ed.), *The Feminine Sacred in South Asia*, Delhi, 1999.
16. V. Strang, *The Meaning of Water, op. cit.*, p. 84, notes: '...water gods or water worship are ubiquitous in ancient mythology ... some of the most well-known deities are associated with alluvial rivers whose floods were critical in the worshippers' inability to produce food'.
17. See K. Lahiri-Dutt, *Fluid Bonds, op. cit.*, ch. 22.
18. C. K. Chapple, *Hinduism and Ecology: The Intersection of Earth, Sky and Water*, Harvard, 2000, pp. xi–xxvii.
19. F. Baartamans, *The Holy Waters: A Primordial Symbol in Hindu Myths*, Delhi, 2000.
20. S. Kumar, *The Puranic Lore of Holy Water-places*, New Delhi, 1983.

Life, Water and Liberation

MARCELO BARROS

'I recognize someone as being of God, not when they talk to me about God, but by the way they talk and act in the affairs of this world.' This was Simone Weil's attitude over 50 years ago.[1] Liberation theology seeks to discern the word and action of God in the great challenges facing the lives of peoples. The core of liberation theology is spirituality. It can be understood as 'the need to imbue the practice of liberation with spirit, that is to say, a concern to unite spirit and the everyday practice of love and solidarity'.[2] True spirituality goes beyond the religious sphere and shows itself in an attitude of love for all creatures. The whole universe is a huge altar on which we can contemplate the presence of God. In church circles and in Christian communities, this ecological spirituality needs to be deepened further. This is a timely and urgent path because the planet's life system is under threat and water is becoming the most precious of resources. Today the crisis of water and care for this natural wonder that capitalism, significantly, reduces to the category of 'water resources' worries the whole of humanity and merits the attention of theology and of Christian and ecumenical spirituality.

I A crisis caused by a model of civilization

Many books and articles have revealed the worrying scale of the world's water crisis.[3] The various international fora devoted to water have shown that one in every two people in the world lives in a home without sewerage and without drinking water at less than a kilometre's distance. Every year, six million poor people, including four million children, die from diseases associated with polluted water.

'According to the studies, the human race still has available around 9000 km^3 of fresh water, a renewable water resource. This is a quantity more than sufficient to supply a population of 20 billion people. The earth currently has a population of 6 billion. However, while the quantity of water available has not changed, human consumption has multiplied almost tenfold in the last century. But humanity has plundered water resources in such a way that the quantity of water available has become insufficient, and is tending to decrease still further.'[4]

Today big multinational companies and local power elites are taking control of water as a commodity and privatizing the sources necessary for human and animal life. Privatization and marketization of waters is a condition imposed by the IMF on poor countries that depend on its loans. All over the world civil society and community groups are organizing to fight this unjust policy. It is a good sign that grass-roots campaigns are being organized against the privatization of municipal water services, and against the construction of monstrous new hydro-electric schemes that destroy the eco-systems of the rivers and do nothing to enhance the lives of the poorest people. These grass-roots campaigns are expressions of citizenship and signs of faith in God, the source of life and love in the universe.[5]

In the Millennium Development Goals, approved by the UN and adopted by 191 member States of the United Nations, there was a proposal 'to reduce by half the percentage of people with no access to safe drinking water and to improve the lives of at least 100 million people living in inadequate housing', and to do so by 2015.[6] The reality is that governments have not succeeded in reaching these objectives, and the situation of poverty and social inequality has deteriorated in recent years. Water constitutes a complex and fragile system with many uses: human nutrition, industrial processes, agriculture, navigation, energy production, recreation and ecology, and others. Almost all known human activities require water. Water is the irreplaceable raw material and currently it is under threat. The civilization that has become dominant in the West in recent centuries is predatory and disrespectful of human beings and nature. Because of this the solution will not come through technical measures alone. We shall have to develop a deeper ecumenical and ecological spirituality that changes the way we look at earth and water and the way we relate to them. In January 2012, various countries suggested that the UN should establish a World Environmental Organization as an independent body to coordinate the response to ecological problems, and specifically to manage water.

II A spiritual relationship with water

From the 1960s the UN started to deal with the issue of water in various international fora and meetings. Various documents and agreements were produced in an attempt to solve the imminent crisis. Anyone who reads these documents will see that there was an attempt to find social, technical and political solutions to the crisis. These measures may help, but they remain within the sphere of the market and don't offer a deeper solution, a relationship of love with the earth and water. This approach has been followed and developed by the religions of forest peoples and by ecumenical spirituality. This doesn't mean lapsing into a fundamentalist sacral vision that denies or diminishes the historical significance of facts and the historical autonomy of the world. Biblical faith invites us to discover the presence and voice of God, not in miracles outside history, but in the facts of life. Ecumenical spirituality teaches us to see signs of the presence and love of God, not by substituting them for historical causes, but in and through those causes. This means that a pluralist liberation theology must re-evaluate these ancient traditions, not to copy them or reproduce them literally, but to learn from them a new, critical attitude of care for water, the earth and all the common goods of the universe.

In all ancient religions water is seen as the source of life and a privileged site of encounter with the Divine. It is not necessary to think that water is a goddess or to believe in legends that make water a human person. We are people of the twenty-first century with a modern, secularized culture, one that therefore has nothing sacral about it. And yet in the elements of earth and in water we can reverence privileged signs of divine love and its affectionate presence in our lives. To develop this spirituality, it is worthwhile remembering points that are common to various religious traditions. We are not recalling these spiritual paths in a confused syncretism, but to enrich our own ecumenical faith with a more universal vision and to receive the loving word God speaks to us through these spiritual approaches.

III Listening to the popular religions of Latin America and Africa[7]

In all religions and spiritual traditions, water has a very rich meaning. Water symbolizes life. In the majority of mythical accounts through which peoples have told the story of the creation of the world, water represents the source of life and the divine energy that gives fruitfulness to the earth and living creatures. The presence of water guarantees life. Indigenous cultures and their faith depend on the environment in which each group lives. An indigenous village in a dry region cannot have the same relationship to water as peoples that were born and live on the banks of a great river. But in both cases water is sacred. All indigenous peoples venerate springs and rivers as places from which life springs. Many initiation rites are performed in the early morning among the waters. In the Amazon region the indigenous communities refer to the Mother of the River as a protective spirit, responsible for the balance of all nature.

Cultures that live in arid regions also venerate water as a hidden treasure for which they long and on which they depend. Rain is seen as sacred water that displays the power of life. There are special drums and beats for the 'rain call'.

Afro-Brazilian religions draw their original inspiration from very ancient African cults, mainly on the Atlantic coast of Africa and the regions to the west. In these areas of Africa, even today, rivers are sacred. Because of this, various names of *orixás* (divine manifestations in Yoruba culture) or *inquices* (the equivalent in Bantu culture) are names of rivers (Oxum, Oyá, Iemanjá and so on). Normally, there is a sacred spring in every temple devoted to the *orixás*. The people venerate every fresh-water spring as the dwelling of Oxum, the manifestation of the divine in female beauty. Water rituals are linked to the moon and to fertility cults. One element common to many cultures of African descent is the interrelation of all the elements of life. The sacred is lived here and now, in all aspects of daily life, and is made manifest in every element of nature. Of these, water is primordial.

IV Water in the culture of biblical Israel[8]

The Bible begins by saying that when God created heaven and earth, the Spirit of God hovered over the waters. All the books of Judaeo-Christian revelation speak of water as a symbol of the Spirit of God that pours out a new life over the universe. God gives the waters of the rain and of the wells to his people as a sign of his covenant of love. The well is the place to which the women of the clans come to fetch water and therefore is the place where the patriarchs meet their wives. By the side of the wells marriages take place and the people make their agreements and swear their oaths (cf. Gen. 24.11ff; Ex. 2.16ff). From biblical times, in many agricultural cultures, whoever controls the water sources and is able to ensure water for all to drink, can govern the people. Even today, in many countries, water is an important factor in governability. According to the book of Exodus, it is through water that God brings his people out of slavery in Egypt into a new, free land. The whole Bible compares the Word of God itself to water that produces life wherever it falls. The Psalms call God the source of living waters and ask him to refresh us with his intoxicating torrents (cf. Ps. 36.9–10; 42.3, etc.).

The biblical prophets associated God with ancient water deities. Various oracles call God a 'spring of pure waters' (Jer. 2.13; cf. Ez. 36.25). These texts invite us to look at a spring and even today see in it a manifestation of God. A disciple of Isaiah said that God would make peace flow for his people like a river overflowing with water (cf. Is. 66.12). After rejecting Israel for betraying the covenant, God agrees to return to the midst of his people like life-giving water (Ezek. 47.1–12).

Rabbinical texts compared the Messiah to the rock from which Moses made water flow in the desert (cf. Ex. 17.1–7; 1 Cor. 10.4). The Messiah was to be the one who gave the people living water in such health-giving abundance that whoever drank it would never be thirsty again. On the basis of this idea John's community developed a catechesis on faith, recalling Jesus' conversation with the Samaritan woman at Jacob's well (John 4). When Jesus tells her that he can give her water that will be a spring of life in her for ever, the woman immediately asks about the Messiah.

From ancient times devout people used to perform ablutions and ritual baths before going on a pilgrimage to the temple ,and when they asked God for a new life. This culture explains John the Baptist's baptismal rite as a sign of repentance, and Christian baptism in that context.

V Behind the gospels

In the 70s CE Mark's gospel reworks a story based on a legend about a struggle between God and the waters. At the beginning, the sea appears as a path that helps people to move from one side to another. Jesus says, 'Let us cross over to the other side of the lake.' Suddenly, during the night, the sea shows itself as the power of the hostile forces the people fear. Jesus talks to the angry waters as a person talks to a living and intelligent being. He orders the wind to stop and the sea to be calm. The text continues: 'The wind dropped and everything was very still'. And the people asked: 'Who ever can he be?—even the wind and the waves do what he tells them!' (Mark 4.35–41).

This is a tradition similar to that of the miraculous catch of fishes. Drawing on Ezekiel (cf. Ezek. 47), Luke describes how Jesus calls some disciples to follow him after a miraculous draught of fishes (Luke 5.1–11). The fourth gospel reproduces a similar story in its last chapter, as a manifestation of the risen Christ in Galilee, calling the disciples once more to their mission (John 21).

According to the fourth gospel, on the last day of the Feast of Tabernacles Jesus says: 'Let anyone who is thirsty come to me, and let the one who believes in me drink. As the scripture has said, "Out of the believer's heart shall flow rivers of living water."' The gospel comments that he was talking about the Holy Spirit that was to be received by all who believed in him (John 7.37–9). Jesus interprets his passion and death on the cross as a baptism (Mark 10.38; Luke 12.50). The fourth gospel stresses the fact that after Jesus' death one of the soldiers pierced his side with a spear, 'and at once blood and water came out' (John 19.34). The water is a sign of the Spirit and the spiritual renewal that God wishes to give to all believers. The victory of Christ and the manifestation of his coming restore creation and reconcile country and city. For the New Jerusalem and the renewed world, there flows from the throne of God and from the Lamb a river of living waters that gives new life to all creatures (cf. Rev. 22.1–3).

VI Created and baptized in water

From the beginning, the Christian churches associated the receiving of the Spirit with the rite of baptism. Paul teaches: 'We have been buried with him by baptism into death, so that, just as Christ was raised from the dead by the glory of the Father, so we too might walk in newness of life' (Rom. 6.4). 'When you were buried with him in baptism, you were also raised with him through faith in the power of God, who raised him from the dead' (Col. 2.12). This energy of love and resurrection active in the person of Jesus has, according to Paul, been hidden for ever in God, in the very act of creating the universe (Eph. 3.9).[9] It is this energy that is expressed in the whole universe as a cosmic body of Christ, the fullness of God's creation (Col. 1.15ff). We are brothers and sisters of God's creation. Creation itself aspires to the freedom of the sons and daughters of God. Salvation and resurrection include people and cosmos. The whole universe participates in human expectation of a full life, to be freed from all that pulls us down, and to receive the inheritance of the sons and daughters of God (Rom. 8).

In the ancient Christian communities, baptism was really a sign of a change of life and the beginning of intimacy with God. It abolished social differences: 'There is no longer Jew or Greek, there is no longer slave or free... for all of you are one in Christ Jesus' (Gal. 3.28). Baptism is like a new flood whose waters wash us clean from the dirt of the flesh and cleanse us, 'not as a removal of dirt from the body, but as an appeal to God for a good conscience, through the resurrection of Jesus Christ' (1 Pet. 3.21). The last promise in the Bible is the water of life that Jesus will give to those who resist and overcome all persecutions (Rev. 22.5ff).

Reading the Bible in this way, in terms of the relationship of God's covenant and the gift of water he guarantees to his people, enables us to think about the reality of water in our world.

VII A macro-ecumenical ministry of waters and life

Pastoral ministry is caring for people in God's name. At the same time, when we see human beings as members of the great community of life, there can be no true and deep care for people without concern for, and engagement with, the nature that surrounds us and with every living creature. Since all living creatures depend on water, care for water becomes an important element of an integrated pastoral ministry.

There can be two forms of water ministry. The first and more important is one that includes an ecological vision of respect and communion with nature in all elements of ministry. This means that in catechesis, in liturgy and all the various sectors of ministry we must always bear in mind care for nature and especially for water. The second form of water ministry is specific and has water as the theme and fundamental concern of pastoral activity.

Since the 1970s, in this area, and in various parts of Latin America, rural workers' pilgrimages have become established. These are 'land pilgrimages' that take place annually in popular sanctuaries or places marked by the martyrdom of comrades. In recent years the pilgrimages have become 'land and water pilgrimages,' and always have a penitential or purification rite on the banks of a river that all pledge themselves to care for. In Petrópolis, in the Brazilian state of Rio Grande do Sul, a community of young people celebrated Lent by holding a pilgrimage every Saturday on the bank of a river, freeing it from the rubbish and the objects thrown into it. For some years in the diocese of Goiás, Bishop Tomás Balduino held the Corpus Christi procession as a walk along the bank of the Rio Vermelho and asked people to adore Christ not only in his eucharistic presence, but as a wounded body in the waters attacked by pollution.

Throughout Latin America, and even beyond, the pastoral letter of Bishop Luis Infanti of Aysen in southern Chile, entitled *Give us this day our daily water* (1 September 2008) had a deep and positive impact. It is an excellent example of how pastoral ministry should take up this cause of defending water at a time when it is threatened by privatization and marketization by the capitalist system.

A few years ago, for communities in regions with a tropical climate, I rewrote the rite of the Easter Vigil, suggesting that the ceremony began on the bank of a local river with a blessing of the waters that would mean not just praise of God but a commitment by the community to defend the river basin. The monks of the Benedictine monastery in Goiás did this for a number of years and the community said that the ritual did more than lectures and other information work to change the attitudes of the people living near the river. Obviously this does not exclude the participation of Christians with other believers and non-believers in environmental defence organizations and river management committees that are now recognized in the constitutions of various Latin American countries.

Water is a universal good and a right of all living creatures. To defend this right is to bear witness that this divine gift cannot be improperly appropriated by some to the detriment of others. This is what makes water a scarce resource. Wadih Awawdé, the current mayor of the Palestinian city of Kafr Kana, the ancient Cana of Galilee, has stated: 'If Jesus came back here today, we would ask him to turn wine into water instead of water into wine.' We cannot do this, but we can campaign together and use ecumenical theology and spirituality to prevent the privatization and marketization of water from being considered normal.

I end this article with a reference to a little-known ecumenical statement that deserves wider publicity. It comes from the Brazilian National Council of Christian Churches, the Federation of Swiss Protestant Churches and the Swiss Bishops' Conference: 'Encouraged by the declarations of the worldwide fellowship of churches on the UN's "Water for Life" international decade for action (2005–2015), we commit ourselves: to convince our churches, congregations, institutions, ecumenical groupings and partner organizations to support this declaration and to pray for its aims; together with the movements and NGOs in Brazil and Switzerland interested in these issues, to motivate public opinion, political forces and the population of our countries to work in favour of the terms set out in this declaration; to lobby the governments of our countries to guarantee, through appropriate laws, the human right to water and the declaration on water as a public good, and to work for the drawing up of an international convention on water to be adopted by the UN.'[10]

Translated by Francis McDonagh

Notes

1. Quoted by Bishop Sebastião Soares in the preface to M. Barros, *O Espírito vem pelas águas*, São Paulo, 2003, p. 5.
2. Jon Sobrino, *Liberación con Espíritu: Apuntes para una nueva espiritualidad*, Santander, 1985, p. 7 (ET: *The Spirituality of Liberation*, New York & London, 1988).
3. Some examples: Ricardo Petrella, *O Manifesto da Água*, Petrópolis, 2002; Demóstenes Romano Filho *et al.*, *Gente cuidando das Águas*, Belo Horizonte, 2002; Marie-France Caïs, Marie-José Del Rey & Jean Pierre Ribaut, *L'Eau et la Vie*, Paris, 1999; Jacques Sironneau, *L'Acqua, Nuovo Obiettivo strategico mondiale*, Trieste, 1997.
4. Cf. Manlio Dinucci, *Il Sistema Globale*, Bologna, 1998, p. 282.
5. For a more detailed treatment of this ecumenical and biblical approach to the spirituality of water, see Marcelo Barros, *O Espírito vem pelas Águas*, São Paulo, 2003.
6. Cf. Juan José Tamayo, *Otra Teología es posible*, Madrid, 2011, p. 112.
7. The bulk of the data on this is taken from Marcelo Barros, *O Espírito vem pelas Águas*, São Paulo, 2003.
8. Marcelo Barros, 'A sede da vida e a água de Deus', *Vida Pastoral* March–April 2006, p. 12.
9. This is the thesis of Adolphe Gesché, *Dieu pour penser*, IV, Paris, 1994.
10. *Ecumenical declaration on water as a human right and a public good*, Berne, 22 April 2005: http://www.oikoumene.org/en/resources/documents/wcc-programmes/justice-diakonia-and-responsibility-for-creation/climate-change-water/water-as-a-human-right-and-a-public-good.html

Part Two: Experiences

Reading the Bible after Fukushima

KUMIKO KATO

I Introduction

The islands that make up Japan are laid out between the continent of Asia and the Pacific Ocean and enjoy the benefits of fresh and salt water. Generous rainfall is a feature of life in Japan. It makes the cultivation of rice possible in irrigated fields, which is the traditional way of growing the national staple. All kinds of products of the sea reach Japan from the waters surrounding the country, where streams from North and South come together. Although excessive rain and snow sometimes cause damage, water remains a gift of nature for Japan. Last year, however, a vast amount of water descended on the country, yet the disasters caused by earthquake and tsunami are not the whole story. Although international interest has focussed on the results of the loss of control at the Fukushima nuclear site, my own experiences extend beyond this event. I begin this article with a short account of the tsunami of 11 March 2011.

II Fixed boundaries break down

The calamitous earthquake in Eastern Japan occurred at 14.46 hrs (2.46 p.m.). After about 30 minutes the giant tsunami up to 20 metres high in parts, hit the Eastern coast of the die Tohoku region. A tectonic plate boundary runs along the Eastern seabed in this area, which has experienced many tsunamis throughout its history and has taken many measures to combat them, such as sea walls, forest fortifications, alarm systems and tsunami drills. This was the area of Japan, and perhaps of the entire world, best protected against tsunamis. But the 2011 tsunami immeasurably outclassed the local authorities' defensive planning. Moreover the first warning underestimated the height of the wave. This resulted in an immense number of dead and missing persons, about 19,300 in all. Once again we discovered that human beings were land creatures in spite of all their technology, and that they would be overwhelmed by water and drown if the boundary between water and earth was breached and water forced its way onto the dry land. For me as a Catholic Christian and exegete, there is a connection between these experiences and new questions to be asked of the Bible and Christian theology.

The biblical creation narrative associates human beings with the living creatures that are to move and dwell on the earth, 'cattle and creeping things and beasts of the earth according to their kinds', made on the sixth day (Gen. 1.24–8). The ancient Israelites described the experience of being in peril of their lives in terms of the dangers of water:

Save me, O God,
for the waters have come up to my neck.
I sink in deep mire, where there is no foothold;
I have come into deep waters
And the flood sweeps over me.
I am weary with my crying;
My throat is parched,
my eyes grow dim with waiting for my God (Ps. 69.2–4).

I hear the cries of the tsunami victims in this psalm. It was a fundamental part of the biblical scriptural belief in creation that God determined and maintained the boundary between water and the earth (cf. Gen. 1.9f.). This notion came from the 'hydrocosmological' conception of creation widespread in Western Asia in ancient times. It held that 'the creation was the product of the combat engaged in by divine power. Its maintenance was a question of holding back the great life-threatening waters'.[1] The theme of struggle is minimized and recedes in Genesis and the emphasis is on God's omnipotence. One psalmist glorifies the work of the Creator thus:

You set the earth on its foundations,
so that it shall never be shaken.
You cover it with the deep as with a garment;
The waters stood above the mountains.
At your rebuke they flee;
At the sound of your thunder they take to flight.

They rose up to the mountains, ran down to the valleys
To the place that you appointed for them.
You set a boundary that they may not pass,
so that they might not again cover the earth (Ps. 104.5–9).

The tsunami shattered this boundary, not for ever, but for a time at least. The young, sick and old died in the water. Many people who tried to carry on with their occupations lost their lives because of their persistence. And then, after the earthquake and tsunami, it snowed in the destroyed area. Not a few of those saved from the waters, old people for the most part, were without gas or electricity and died from cold in emergency shelters. Christians might well have asked whether the Creator had abandoned those of his creatures made to live on land, including humans. Could this be some kind of punishment, like the flood of ancient times (Gen. 6—9)? In fact it happened during Lent, and like Job and together with him, Christians in their churches cried out to God and bewailed the results of this disaster which had killed so many innocent creatures.

III Poisoned land, poisoned water

In April the air temperature rose and new leaves appeared on some of the trees that had escaped the effects of the black waters. The traces of greenery among the muddy debris were reminiscent of the fresh olive leaf which the dove brought back to Noah in the Ark: 'But God remembered Noah and all the wild animals and all the domestic animals that were with him in the ark. And God made a wind blow over the earth, and the waters subsided' (Gen. 8.1). 'He waited another seven days, and again he sent out the dove from the ark; and the dove came back to him in the evening, and there in its beak was a freshly plucked olive leaf' (Gen. 8.11).

As long as 'cold and heat, summer and winter, day and night, shall not cease' (Gen. 8.22), there is hope, however long it takes to get rid of the debris, to devise new plans and rebuild towns and villages. At least, we might have affirmed that most readily if the nuclear disaster had not occurred in Fukushima. It changed our situation fundamentally.

From 11 to 12 March 2011, while rescue teams carried on searching for missing persons and tried to distribute drinking water and rations in more than 1,000 emergency facilities, the Fukushima nuclear power station affected by the earthquake and tsunami lost all its cooling systems and went out of control. Three reactors suffered core meltdowns, which we were told initially was no more than a possibility. The government decreed the evacuation of about 85,000 inhabitants from an area of 20 km around the nuclear power station. Most of these people took no possessions with them when they left their homes, for they thought it was merely a short-term precautionary measure. The search for tsunami victims was abandoned in this area. Not a few of the old people evacuated from hospitals and homes for the aged died during the badly-organized transport or soon afterwards. A large amount of livestock, including bullocks, cows, pigs and poultry, kept in the 20-km zone, died from hunger and thirst after the evacuation. Some of the cattle that slipped their halters still live as wild animals in the forbidden zone. This and the areas added later are still restricted because the radiation there exceeds the reference level of 20 millisievert per annum recommended by the International Commission on Radiological Protection (ICRP). Such things are characteristic of the nightmare situation in the prohibited zone. But people are suffering even outside that area. Almost half the prefecture of Fukushima is contaminated. Although the radiation does not exceed the value registered in the restricted zone, it is much higher than normal. The people there, especially those with young children, are faced with a difficult decision. They do not know whether to stay or to leave the area they know so well and the basis of their everyday lives.

The radioactive substances released from the nuclear power station have poisoned forests, rivers, lakes and the sea, and therefore the water cycle of the entire world.

IV Many voices are raised against the single voice of hubris

The creation hymn that I have already quoted commemorates the water cycle maintained by the Creator which bestows life on people and animals alike:

> You make springs gush forth in the valleys;
> They flow between the hills,
> giving drink to every wild animal;

the wild asses quench their thirst.
By the streams the birds of the air have their habitation;
They sing among the branches.
From your lofty abode you water the mountains;
The earth is satisfied with the fruit of your work.
You cause the grass to grow for the cattle,
and plants for people to use,
to bring forth food from the earth (Ps. 104.10–14).

The landscape in the prefecture of Fukushima (which means 'happy land' in Japanese) is similar to that celebrated in the psalm. Who is responsible for the destruction of the land and the contamination of the global water cycle? Although I do not insist on the collective guilt of the people of Japan, we are no longer in the position of Job protesting his innocence before the Creator (cf. Job 31).

As is generally acknowledged, nuclear energy is a technology closely associated with nuclear weapons. Since 1954, the Japanese State (which neither has nor may possess nuclear weaponry) has devoted a considerable budget to a national project for research into nuclear energy and its application. The ambition of the politicians committed to this project was and remains that it should give the State the scientific and technical potential to produce nuclear weapons. This nuclear policy, which obtained no consensus among the people of Japan, was concealed behind the motto 'atoms for peace'. With politicians' support, a firmly-closed system came into being. This system comprised state research institutes, private nuclear industrialists and nuclear engineers. None of these took the risks of accidents and nuclear-waste problems seriously or felt responsible for any accidents. After all, any such person was already excluded from the system. In spite of all foreign and domestic accidents, the same policy had always prevailed, so that new nuclear power stations were built on sites and in a country subject to multiple earthquakes.[2]

The Hebrew Bible tells the story of the city-state of Babel, which had only one tongue and had developed an advanced technology and defence system: 'Now the whole earth had one language and the same words' (Gen. 11.1). There was only one voice in the land, and no objections to it were heard. Everyone agreed: '"Come, let us build ourselves a city, and a tower with its top in the heavens, and let us make a name for ourselves; otherwise we shall be scattered abroad upon the face of the whole earth'

(Gen. 11.4). The walled city was the supreme form of defence in biblical times. But the Creator thwarted the plans of the people of Babel, not by force but by multiplying their form of self-expression. I am convinced that in present-day Japan we too need a multiplication of languages. We need many voices to speak out against the single voice of the system. The nuclear disaster has to break open the system in Japan, or we shall offer a example to the world that will prove far worse than Babel.

There are many connections between the experiences of the tsunami and of nuclear catastrophe and the Hebrew Bible. The Israelites also lived on the periphery of the world's first great civilizations, suffered the devastation of war and natural disasters, reflected on them, and handed on their experiences. 'Remembrance' was their duty.

Remember Hiroshima, Nagasaki and Fukushima, but also remember Three Mile Island, Chernobyl and Fukushima.

If we duly recall these names and the associated events, 'it may be that the Lord, the God of hosts, will be gracious' to us [the remnant of Joseph] (cf. Amos 5.15).

Translated by J. G. Cumming

Notes

1. Othmar Keel and Silvia Schroer, *Schöpfung. Biblische Theologien im Kontext altorientalischer Religionen*, Göttingen, 2002, p. 184.

2. Hitoshi Yoshioka, *Genshiryoku no Shakaishi. Sono Nihonteki Tenkai* [A social history of atomic energy in Japan], Tokyo, 2011.

The Bridge of Mostar

ŽELJKO IVANKOVIĆ

I Introduction

For generations we have grown used to thinking of Bosnia-Herzegovina as a country of mountains and rivers, difficult to cross and conquer. The partisan rhetoric of World War II and the Cold War was rekindled by Yugoslav war films that repeatedly show bridges being blown up. On the other hand, our policy of 'non-alignment' and 'peaceful co-existence between nations', followed by reading Ivo Andrić, our winner of the Nobel Prize for Literature, led us to discover the full practical significance and symbolic value of bridges, which is as much physical as spiritual. It also brought home to us the need to keep building them on the historic sites where cultures and civilizations meet, as in the Balkans and Bosnia.

Bridges have made our country navigable, brought us closer together, and have become symbolic in themselves of opening up to otherness and difference. Throughout history, rivers were often the real borders between disparate parts of Bosnia-Herzegovinan society, which were divided by their religions, nationalities and cultures. Bridges too were more than physical means of communication.

These rivers, and these real and symbolic border areas, did not begin to free themselves from ideological labels and rigid divisions, and even from conflicts, until the time of the general democratization of Bosnia-Herzegovina, subjected until then to a clash of civilizations. Henceforth the terms used would become more desirable and pleasing, such as 'the intersection of the world's great civilizations'. In short, bridges were conducive to meetings between, and the coexistence of, (Orthodox and Catholic) Christians, Muslims and Jews. Rivers defined the divisions, and bridges signified an historic victory over the divisions, even if, unfortunately, they were often temporary. Rivers were a permanent element, and bridges signified the triumph of weakness over durability. Therefore it might be said that the gradual historic fusion of Bosnia-Herzegovina was carried out by the syncretic process of physical and spiritual bridge building.

The celebrated bridges of the Yugoslav writer Ivo Andrić, especially the bridge of the city of Višegrad in his novel *The Bridge on the Drina*, have become so to speak literary monuments of the architecture and meeting of differences. They also implicitly recall all the conflicts throughout a long historical period, during which river and bridge, simultaneously separable and potentially contradictory, have always played the same traditional parts. The river appears as a symbol of natural forces and time that can never be regained; whereas the bridge's essential character has been its taming of this force of the waters by its own human and temporal capacities. In a country with so many waterways and rivers, which, though not extensive, are very 'beautiful', and in a country with so many historic changes, which, though not so very 'fine', have proved very extensive, the places where bridges have spanned rivers are few in number, although this makes them special. Nevertheless, roundabout the bridges, the forces of destruction always seemed more powerful than the forces of construction. Even though the famous Bridge over the Drina, the *pars pro toto* of all our bridges, was the focus of all the controversies of the turbulent centuries of Bosnia-Herzegovina's existence, the Mostar Bridge, the most famous in this part of the world, remained aloof from all conflict. It endured in all its beauty and elegance, and architectural design and finish, as a place of inspiration for artists and lovers of beauty, and in its biological quasi-symbiosis with the magnificent River Neretva.

II A contested bridge

The Austrian writer and traveller Robert Michel once wrote: 'if I had to say which was the most beautiful bridge in the world, the bridge of my choice would probably be the Old Bridge of Mostar'. At present, the only 'conflicts' affecting it are mainly matters of aesthetic debates between painters and poets, travel writers and architects. There are debates whether the Old Bridge is 'the linked rainbow' or 'the crescent moon' or 'Apollo–a god loved among gods'...

The Old Bridge was not 'contested' until 1993. In the sixteenth century, on the site of a former wooden bridge dating back to before 1452, the Turkish architect Mimar Hajrudin Aga took nine years to build the stone bridge, 29 metres long, and with an arch 12 metres wide, as a testimony to the amount of traffic crossing the river Neretva and the economic strength that it engendered. Evliya Čelebija, an Ottoman Turkish writer, says of the name of the town: 'The town of Mostar means a town with its bridge'. The town took its name from *mostari* – the guardians of the bridge in the town, *civitas pontis*. The name is mentioned for the first time in 1468–9, during Ottoman rule, when it is described as a small town with two towers on the two sides of the bridge. The town and its bridge have linked their destiny, courageously and nobly overhanging the Neretva, and welcoming and watching empires and States leave.

Nevertheless, even if the Old Bridge offers no evidence of any dispute, this does not mean that Mostar, and Bosnia as a whole, are places where an idyllically diverse life is possible. In fact, the different national, cultural and religious communities bear the marks of the traumatic experiences of different periods of history. Under the Ottoman Empire, Christians suffered from inequalities, then, with the arrival of the Austro-Hungarian Empire, it was the Muslims who experienced fear and insecurity. Mostar was to suffer turbulent demographic changes during the Kingdom of Yugoslavia and during Tito's Yugoslavia, but it always represented the centre of what the binominal name 'Bosnia-Herzegovina' stands for: not only the geographical nature but the difference, the otherness, of Bosnia. Mostar is its central location, the town on the river Neretva that divides it into its own East and West.

With the 1993 war, the town was divided into East and West both politically and militarily, for the first time in its history. One year after the start of the war, even though Mostar and its citizens had experienced the devastation wrought by invading troops at the beginning of May 1993, the Bosnian–Croatian conflict began in Mostar, culminating in the vandalism of the destruction of the Old Bridge on 9 November 1993.

III   Total marginality

As I said, under Ottoman Turkish domination Bosnia-Herzegovina became the contact-point of several religious and cultural entities, and these denominational groups lived almost all the time side-by-side in four very distinctive societies. As Fernand Braudel remarks: 'Civilization and culture are the oceans of routine'. They lived in entirely marginal spheres, ghettoized in a world far distant from the vast and 'oceanic' cultural, historical and social changes occurring in the rest of the world. The accentuation of divisions and differences culminated in the bloodbaths of the Second World War, and became more pronounced after the victory of Tito's military and political option. At a political gathering in Mostar, one of Tito's generals, lacking education but imbued with the spirit of Communist ideology, declared when refusing to divide Herzegovina in accordance with the East–West axis: 'No division! There aren't two banks; there's only one!'

Like the one it followed, this declaration (which, even today, makes us laugh until we cry) did not abolish the divisions, but just swept them under the carpet and anaesthetized them under the threat of ideological terror. Instead of working to heal memory and treat historical traumas, we have merely perpetuated the ideological mantras of Yugo-Communism. Revolutionary and ideological persecution, the lack of criminal trials after the Second World War, the failure to broach national questions, ignorance of human rights and freedoms, and general Communist ideologization have all bounced back in recent events like a poisoned boomerang. With the fall of the Berlin wall, Ina Merdjanova's idea that 'the national ideology remained a central element of culture under Communism', and that to ignore the national question in the name of class ideology or all supranational ideology, was a fatal error, has been confirmed.

Perhaps the words that Ivo Andrić puts into the mouth of one of his heroes are true: 'But in Bosnian civil society there was always a phoney middle-class politeness, an advised form of self-deception and deception of others by means of high-sounding phrases and futile ceremonies. Perhaps this hid the hatred, but it neither suppressed it nor prevented it from growing'.

The finest instances of religious tolerance, that reigned for 100 years in Bosnia-Herzegovina, disappeared in an instant like soap bubbles.

IV Memories, symbols and destruction

Before the last war, collective memories (especially the most negative in historical experience), overwhelmed by reality and shattered by changes in the social paradigm, were infected by the inclusion of mythomania in collective awareness. Collective memories were full of an unrevised past, loaded with new constructions and flooded with the alluvia of fictive waters. They lost track of what was true in memories, and the capacity to distinguish old from new myths and recognize the daily deposits of suspended manipulatory and ideological material. 'How much harm we do with our false memories!/ The just sword of memory often severs the very good it seeks to defend'(the words of the Croatian Protestant theologian Miroslav Volf). This was illustrated by the soldier representing one ethnic group and denomination who recently finished reading *The Bridge on the Drina*, brandished the book before a foreign journalist's camera, and 'explained and justified' his act of war against another group and religion. Then there was the general who, when he entered Srebrenica, recalled the vengeance taken for defeats undergone during battles described in romantic verse epics.

I cannot remember anyone before this brandishing national and religious symbols, searching literature for 'arguments' to justify destruction, and then using fictional events as an alibi for the crime. The political tsunami launched by the fall of the Iron Curtain did not stop when the monuments of Communism were demolished, and the names of towns and streets were changed. But in its destructive course it penetrated more deeply into history, destroying religious and cultural monuments that had lasted for many centuries.

The words of the Croatian writer Dubravka Ugrešić confirmed the fact that 'Devastation is never solely material; it has multiple aspects, multiple meanings, ambiguous but always definitive'. We can 'understand' that so many buildings with a symbolic commemorative meaning have been destroyed (the National Library of the University and the Oriental Institute of Sarajevo, the Ferhadija Mosque of Banja Luka, the Aladža Mosque in Foča, the Žitomislić Monastery, the Old Bridge of Mostar) rather than mere infrastructures. Doubtless this destruction attained the objective of 'vengeance, humiliation and repression of undesirable ways of thinking' (the German historian Alexander Demandt), by attacking especially buildings without any use-value as far as collective memories were concerned. The Czech writer Milan Kundera says that these acts of vandalism create the new masters of the present and the future, by establishing an ambiance apt to favour the creation of another past. It was in a similarly vitiated atmosphere that an eminent specialist in the culture of one nation and religious group rejoiced that all Sarajevo was on fire, and a truck driver in the process of destroying the city of Dubrovnik cynically promised that, when the task was done, he would rebuild it to look 'even older and more beautiful'.

V An ambitious project

The international community wanted the Bridge of Mostar in its new manifestation to be older and more attractive. This planned 'restoration' of the Old Bridge was one of UNESCO's most ambitious and most prestigious projects among its efforts to construct a replica of a lost heritage. The replica was presented to Mostar and Bosnia-Herzegovina at an opening ceremony on 23 July 2004. The town was to recover the symbol which made it identifiable all over the world. The partisan general announced that there was now a single bank where there had been two before. The bridge might have linked the two sides again, but it has not united the people.

After all, in order to experience a truly collective idyll, another project would have been necessary, like the one imposed in Germany after its defeat, and designated with the three famous 'Ds': de-Nazification, demilitarization and democratization – to which, of course, we have to add the Marshall Plan. A project of similar scope would have been needed to make sure of beginning the approach to a complete long-term reconstruction of society, and, by cleansing the memory of general social negligence, to the construction of modern dialogue in an open society. All that would have been necessary to ensure the destruction of stereotypes and illusions about one's own justice and the iniquity of others. But, instead of introducing this essential plan, peace-maintenance activities were multiplied, and certain actions of top-ranking political and religious personalities fed mutual mistrust and encouraged post-conflict trauma. But what was needed was what the society of Bosnia-Herzegovina never had: the achievement of an open and responsible pluralist society.

The tragic truth is that in Mostar and Bosnia-Herzegovina we are still in a state of war after war, a war of countless tedious demarcations of territory. People are consumed by ludicrous rivalries: Who will build the most religious buildings on the territory of Bosnia-Herzegovina? Who will erect the highest cross and the most easily visible church tower or minaret – veritable 'watchtowers' and posts declaring one's group's defiance of another? Those in power, politicians and religious authorities, jostle each other before the public to justify themselves by means of renationalization, re-Islamization or re-Christianization. But all this contributes to yet another radicalization of the social fabric of Bosnia-Herzegovina, which is still desperately pre-modern and split. Those who imagine that they are dealing with a nation of believers are indeed deceived by appearances.

Instead of the division formerly defined by rivers, the borders are now marked out by new religious buildings. Bridges may have been able to surmount territorial divisions, but the current social divisions are still waiting for their bridges. Those who have used the Dayton Peace Agreements to bring the war to an end, and have neglected all the other necessary battles, seem merely to have introduced new problems. We should heed the Argentinian writer Julio Cortazar in his novel *Marelle (Hopscotch)* and unmask the false order of the West. We need to run scared from its stalemates and blind alleys, its fragmentation of reality, its false dichotomies, its conformism, and its abstractions. But instead we are still where we were before. We can see the other bank clearly from time to time, but we cannot swim across the 'metaphysical river', and no meeting with the other side has been achieved.

After the investment of millions of dollars and enormous hopes in the rebuilding of the bridge, the noblest end is almost in sight atop the Bridge of Mostar. But the wounds of history are still untreated. In too great haste to restore the architectural and physical heritage, we have forgotten the Bridge's immaterial heritage: its promise of reconciliation and the echo of its 'dangerous memories'. And not only in Mostar!

Translated by Felicity Leng

WATER in Action

MARY E. HUNT

I Introduction

The Women's Alliance for Theology, Ethics and Ritual (WATER) is 'an international community of justice-seeking people who promote the use of feminist religious values to make social change'.[1] The name, like the work involved, is intended to have many layers of meaning, ripples and streams of action. The Alliance was founded in 1983 by a small group of women in the Washington, DC area. It now has a strong international presence on the internet and in feminist spiritual, religious, and political circles. Like other forms of water, WATER the organization faces challenges endemic to its mission. A partial account of the history of WATER, its current priorities, and some of its future plans should make this clear.

II The history of WATER

In the early 1980s, feminist work in religion was beginning to take hold in some countries, to such an extent that a backlash began to develop against previous gains. For example, inclusive language became increasingly controversial; women ministers and rabbis were emerging as powerful leaders challenging the patriarchal *status quo*; and feminist scholars were publishing materials that called prevailing theological models into question. Nevertheless, the theological establishment in the United States would not change sufficiently to make room for a significant number of feminist scholars, and it was soon evident that the most outspoken, critical, and creative thinkers would find no room at the theological inn. Women had to create rooms of their own, in the manner of Virginia Woolf, if they were to bring their insights to fruition.

I had just moved to Washington, DC, after two years of teaching and activism in Argentina. I was a young scholar with plenty of energy and enthusiasm for creating the kinds of 'new space' recommended by the feminist philosopher Mary Daly. As an out lesbian who was pro-choice, I realized that my job options in Catholic theological academia were limited, and that that women needed their own organizations or institutions in order to work unfettered by the demands of tenure in the university and of orthodoxy in the Church. Encouraged by the example of women who had formed NETWORK: A National Catholic Social Justice Lobby,[2] I dreamed of a similar collective effort by women in the field of religion.

In August 1992, I wrote a three-page proposal for a Women's Theological Alliance calling for 'an ecumenical women's effort to do justice and deepen the many faiths through theological reflection.' I shared it with colleagues. Enthusiasm was immediate: we would be much stronger together than alone. A typically American 'can do' attitude made a naïve idea a reality, even without a penny to pay for it.

A dozen Protestant and Catholic women scholars and ministers (including *Concilium* writers Mary Collins, Madonna Kolbenschlag and Elisabeth Schüssler Fiorenza) gathered to discuss the idea. From the start, as women scholars and activists joined forces to bring about religiously-informed social change in accordance with a feminist programme, the Alliance was to have dual citizenship in the academy and in the activist realm. We did not wish simply to include women, feature female voices, and bring women's perspectives into previously all-male conversations. Instead, we had an explicitly feminist agenda based on the assumption that women, like all marginalized people, are full human beings with communicable insights bearing on the creation of a just and equitable world.

The day after the initial meeting, I joked with my partner, a liturgist and therapist, that if we added 'ethics and ritual' we could call this fledgling organization WATER. It has been WATER ever since. This happy acronym articulates, both in a word and spelled out, what we are: Women (although some feminist men have always formed part of our movement); an Alliance that operates as a clearing-house for ideas, a web of communication, and a source of support for projects and publications; Theology, in the broadest sense of the term encompassing issues of ultimate meaning and value; Ethics, as an explicit commitment to use feminist religious insights to bring about change; and Ritual, a range of ways of embodying life passages, everyday experiences, and commitments, and raising them to the point of public expression. Thus WATER was born.

The biblical image of justice rolling down like water (Amos 5.24) was an immediate association for us. But we also thought of the waters of birth that, for so many women, were eclipsed by the waters of baptism in patriarchal Christianity. It was only in later years that we ventured beyond Christian and Jewish images to learn about Hindu cleansing rituals, for example, and that Muslim women believe that creation is the process by which 'We' (the Divine) 'made every living thing of water' (Qur'an 21.30 [Dawood]). Water has figured centrally in many of our rituals and prayers. It reminds us regularly that many women in the world still spend a great part of their day carrying clean water to their families, and that our work is to change this situation.

The downside of such an appealing name is that we get regular calls from people trying to telephone the local water company, often when their water has been turned off for not paying the bill. We keep the company's number handy to give to them, but each call reminds us that the real work of WATER is to create a world in which the human right to water does not depend on an individual's ability to pay for it.

III WATER's priorities

As WATER completes the third decade of its work, our priorities reflect the dynamics of a world that seems to be less just and less equal than when we started our group 30 years ago. Perhaps we are simply more aware of the complexity of the injustice represented by water haves and have-nots. The South African theologian Steve de Gruchy describes the situation in his essay 'Dealing with Our Own Sewage: Spirituality and Ethics in the Sustainability Agenda': 'Our thinking about sustainability must deal with sewage because we have to live with our waste. It cannot leave the globe. It hangs around and it comes back to haunt us. Previous civilizations may have got away with flushing the problem downstream, but in a globalized world there is no downstream, or, more correctly: 'we all live downstream'. There is one stream of water from which we all drink, and any sustainable world has to come to terms with this fact.[3]

Knowing that women and dependent children are always 'downstream' in an unjust world, WATER's current work is more focussed than ever on how to bring feminist religious commitments to bear on working for social change. For instance, our Feminist Liberation Theologians' Network meets annually to marshal the resources of scholars and activists and influence theological education and public policy toward more inclusive ends.[4] Our liturgy and meditation groups recharge the batteries of those engaged in working for social change.[5]

Our monthly teleconferences are open to all and available later on our website. They are attractive learning experiences on feminist themes.[6] Recent offerings included contributions from scholar and activists, including Shawn Copeland on 'Enfleshing Freedom: Body, Race, and Being', Gale Yee on 'Where are you really from? An Asian American feminist biblical scholar reflects on her guild,' Rita Nakashima Brock on 'Occupying paradise,' and Rosemary Radford Ruether on 'Feminist theology in theological education.' Many of these events were based on chapters by authors and speakers in WATER's latest publication, *New Feminist Christianity: Many Voices, Many Views*.[7]

Coalition work with like-minded groups combines our energies. Recent examples include a working meeting, co-sponsored with Call to Action,[8] of Catholic feminist thought leaders to analyze and strategize about the current difficult situation for all Catholics in a kyriarchal Church. WATER also collaborated on a powerful retreat for Catholic lesbian women co-directed with the Women of Dignity USA, the Catholic LGBTIQ advocacy and support group.[9]

WATER is part of the Women-Church Convergence,[10] 'a coalition of autonomous Catholic-rooted organizations/groups raising a feminist voice and committed to an ecclesia of women which is participative, egalitarian and self-governing'. As such, we seek to support the many ways that Catholic feminists, including nuns, bring their resources to bear on the needs of the world. We also work ecumenically and interreligiously.

Our agenda includes training future generations of feminist scholars, ministers, and activists. We have interns and visiting scholars who join our team to learn how to run the business side of a non-profit organization, and to add their work to the ideological mix. We also offer pastoral counselling and psychotherapy from a feminist perspective, since dealing with the needs of individuals struggling with life's problems is an important part of social change.

IV   WATER's future plans

WATER's future work remains to be defined but the trajectory is clear. We seek to reverse the flow of resources toward the wealthy and powerful and to rechannel it towards the common good. We continue to be a place where people can attend programmes, borrow books, sit in prayer, explore ideas, try out new thoughts, and expect quality research and writing coupled with a preferential option for the marginalized.

We shall deepen our commitment to international and interfaith collaboration, and rely on technology to connect us beyond our imaginings. The next generation of leadership at WATER will undoubtedly be far more multi-racial, multi-ethnic and multi-religious than the early staff. We expect that the theo-ethical agenda that began with a focus on the well-being of women and children will expand exponentially to encompass current anti-racism, pro-LGBTIQ, and ecofeminist concerns, and go far beyond those parameters to a cosmic consciousness that reflects new scientific discoveries as they relate to feminist work in religion.

We hope that our legacy for years to come will be our commitment to bring feminist religious values to the shaping of a just cosmos. Then many more people, like the woman in Samaria and so many feminist women and men today, will be given this water and 'never be thirsty again' (John 4.15).

Notes

1. See http://www.waterwomensalliance.org/.
2. See www.networklobby.org.
3. Steve de Gruchy, 'Dealing with Our Own Sewage: Spirituality and Ethics in the Sustainability Agenda', Address to the World Forum on Theology and Liberation, Belém, Brazil, January 2009, p. 4. http://www.wftl.org/pdf/066.pdf. Ironically and sadly, de Gruchy died in a river accident near the Drakenberg Mountain (Mooi River) in February 2010.
4. See http://www.waterwomensalliance.org/feminist-liberation-theologians-network/.
5. See http://www.waterwomensalliance.org/spirituality-series/.
6. See http://www.waterwomensalliance.org/teleconferences/.
7. M. E. Hunt & D. L. Neu (eds), *New Feminist Christianity: Many Voices, Many Views*, Woodstock, VT, 2010.
8. See http://www.cta-usa.org/.
9. See http://www.dignityusa.org/.
10. See http://www.women-churchconvergence.org/.

Making Peace with Water

LUIS INFANTI DE LA MORA OSM

I Editors' preface

The Chilean population of Aysen has been protesting for many months (2011–12) in the extreme South of the American continent. They are defending their water against regional hydro-electric projects, and propose instead a development in harmony with divine creation. The Apostolic Vicariate of Aysen, presided over by Bishop Infanti, joined in the peaceful protests and backed the proposals of civil society. This led to harsh criticisms by the Chilean government authorities, so the Bishop wrote a letter quoting his opponents' words: 'Let the Bishop stick to praying!'. He said: 'I can assure you that during all these days of conflict, all over Aysen many thousands of people (including me) have been praying... demanding justice, fairness and dignity for our people' (9 March 2012). A few years earlier (1 September 2008), he had published his prophetic document *Give us this day our daily* water, which had international repercussions.

II An abundance of water

Even though water figures largely in the Bible, the sacraments, the life of Jesus and our own lives, I had not really paid it much attention until about seven years ago. I always thought of it as one more element among others, perhaps because in my life I was always surrounded by an abundance of water, especially in Aysen, where we enjoy giant glaciers (Northern and Southern ice fields), abundant rainfall, countless rivers, waterfalls and tumultuous seas.

This abundance of water in Patagonia attracted powerful international companies to plan hydro-electric mega-projects, without considering the input of the local population, who for many long years had endured great strain and sacrifices in their efforts to 'make a country' in frequently inhospitable regions. Consequently, these mega-projects gave rise to opposing visions and growing tensions in local communities and villages. As the Church, we felt the need to take part in these debates; we wanted to bring ethical and spiritual considerations into the dialogue and to discern more deeply and calmly what was happening to us.

That process of church discernment led to the writing of a Pastoral Letter (*Give us this day our daily water,* 2008), and to a very enriching and stimulating exchange with environmental, political, economic, social, cultural and, of course, religious sectors, and with indigenous peoples (Mapuches, Huilliches, Tehuelches). We thought it was essential to ask how much water we had; how we used it; who owned it; what laws controlled it; why there was so much interest in water from transnational companies; what significance water had in our lives and spirituality, in the Bible, and for the various peoples and religions of the earth; what benefits or damage might come from these mega-projects; how we imagined the future of our region and of our children in the years to come; and so on.

III Powerful interests

This inquiry also helped us also to understand the major interests of the bottled-water businesses, the powerful interests and links between water and energy, mining, agribusiness, forest enterprises, fishing, tourism, health and so forth. In particular, it helped us to consider from the perspective of water the world we were building, the powers (and struggles) occurring in this area, the sufferings and distress caused to people by a scarcity or absence of water, and what kind of input people should have in decisions that are or ought to be taken about water. In all these questions, we realized that ethics and spirituality were crucial, because they spoke to the conscience and reached the heart of life or death for every human being, and every living creature (plants, animals, food, and so on).

All this comes from a fundamental, original, traditional faith of the People of God: 'The earth and water are from God'. He is the Creator, the master, the owner of every being and every element in creation. Every creature is as it is to the extent that it reaches the fulfilment and perfection of its being, according to the purpose for which the Creator created it. God entrusted humanity from its creation with the great responsibility to look after and enable each creature to reach fulfilment. Accordingly, human beings should try to make a tree, an animal or the environment, in general and in particular, achieve perfection.

But what about human beings themselves? A total vision of faith leads us to seek their fulfilment as sons and daughters of God, as Christ insisted: 'Be perfect as my Father in heaven is perfect' (that is, as God is perfect as God, so you should be perfect as what you are: persons). In this process of perfection, human rights and the Gospel are an integral part of our faith and pastoral care.

We feel that the kind of anthropocentric vision so strongly promoted and favoured at the moment is scarcely biblical. It might also lead to injury to humans themselves, for, when they are considered as the centre and lords of all creation, we sacrifice creation itself in order to satisfy their needs and even desires, thereby seriously harming human life too.

This is what we find in a consumer society in which the riches of nature are increasingly exploited and despoiled, so that so much is wasted (how much food is thrown away in 'developed' societies?). Furthermore, large sectors of humanity are deprived of these common goods, so that millions of people are condemned to poverty, suffering and even death. Indeed, experts calculate that 1000 million people currently lack sufficient access to drinking water, and 860 million suffer from hunger. It is no accident that 20 per cent of the world population controls and consumes 80 per cent of all natural resources: there are policies and powers that plan this. It would appear that the policies of many States are governed by a very inhuman, unethical and immoral principle, which we could express thus: 'We can't eliminate poverty, so let's eliminate the poor'.

IV Our responsibility and task

There are some common goods which are indispensable and essential to the life of every human being and every living thing. These are water, air and the earth. Deprivation of these is ultimately life-threatening. Today this deprivation is largely promoted and carried out by neo-liberal policies, which lead to privatization and even commercialization of these essential goods. Certain large transnational companies take them over, always sacrificing the poorest and most defenceless people, by denying them access to these goods (children are always the first victims).

If God the Creator is the lord of every created being, and human beings are called to look after them, it is wrong that some people or companies should take possession of these goods and decide which people to benefit and which to eliminate. Here we should pay great attention to a strong statement by Pope John Paul II in Puebla (Mexico) in 1979: 'There is a social mortgage on all private property' (Third General Conference of the Latin American Bishops, No. 1224).

Today vast areas of the planet lack water. In others there are serious and growing conflicts about its use between human consumption, agriculture, mining, industry, hydro-electricity and tourism. To whom should we give priority? Should economic interests prevail in these decisions? What parts do ethics and spirituality play here?

I believe that our faith offers us a very important function in promoting and influencing a new water culture, a new deal for caring, respecting and communion with natural goods, feeling them to be an essential and integral part of our lives, as living beings that share with humans one same beginning and end. Through our faith we must more actively seek peace with water and the environment.

As the People of God, we have a responsibility and an urgent task: to make peace with water. We need new St Francises for today, so that, with 'Sister Water and Sister Earth', we can build new heavens and new earths, and have life, abundant life.

Translated by Dinah Livingstone

Part Three: Theological Forum

Kateri Tekakwitha: the First Indigenous Saint of North America

BERNADETTE RIGAL-CELLARD

I Introduction

On 19 December 2011 the Pope authorized the promulgation of the decree recognizing the miracle atributed to the intercession of Kateri Tekakwitha (1656–80), and on 18 February 2012 her canonization was announced for 21 October 2012, when she was duly canonized. Her cause was introduced in 1884 in the United States, where she was born, then in Canada, where she died. These unique circumstances made her a bi-national saint. Accordingly, Stephen Harper, the Canadian Prime Minister, said of her forthcoming canonization: 'It will be a great day for Canadian Catholics and a very great honour for our country' (20 February 2012).

By becoming the first indigenous saint of North America, Kateri raised her Amerindian people to the level of the other peoples of Catholic faith and strengthened universal recognition of the North American church. In spite of an expansion and vitality unique in the West (43 per cent Canadians and around 25 per cent Americans are Catholics), this church has not been rewarded, so to speak, by the canonization of a due proportion of its members. Until Kateri, its very few saints were all Americans of European descent, or were even born in Europe.

Examining the issues involved in Kateri's canonization reveals the complexity of relations between the Church and indigenous Americans, and the latter's organizational capacities. These have enabled them to affirm their identity at the heart of the Roman institution and among indigenous traditionalists, or those who have become members of one or other Protestant denomination[1]. Around 55 per cent of Native Canadians out of 1.3 million are thought to be Roman Catholics. Although 29 per cent of Native Americans in the United States were Catholics in the 1940s, the present proportion is no more than 17 per cent, or about 500,000 Catholics out of 2,475,965 Native Americans). Nevertheless, it is difficult to check the accuracy of these figures, since Federal statistics do not mention religion and many dioceses do not know the ethnic origins of all their members. There are considerable regional variations, and the baptized are counted but the figures do not take regular practice into account.

II A national model

Tekakwitha was born near Auriesville, NY. Her Algonquin mother had been evangelized, but not her Iroquois Mohawk father. They died during a smallpox epidemic. The young child survived but was left weak and scarred. She went to live with her uncle. Jesuits who met her were surprised by her behaviour and her Catholic faith and called her the Lily of the Agniers (Agniers was a French term for the Mohawks). She asked to be baptized, went through a protracted period of initiation, and was baptized as Catherine on Easter Day 1676. She dedicated herself to Jesus, refused to marry and lived as required by the religious model of the time. She re-joined the Catholic Iroquois at the mission of Sault-Saint-Louis, near Montreal (now Kahnawake). There she followed a life of penitence and prayer and died when 24 years of age, 'in the odour of sanctity'. Local tradition records various miracles due to her intercession.

At the end of the nineteenth century, when the US clergy were searching for national models, the story of Catherine/Kateri the Native American, was revived, and her cause was introduced. Pius XII made her Venerable in 1943, after compilation of the positio recording her virtues. Subsequently, Kateri benefited from the procedure for older causes, that is, those whose candidates lived so long ago that testimonies could not be subjected to the same criteria required of contemporary candidates. The facts as reported were assessed as miraculous. The Postulator produced three files on these manifestations, the *positiones super miris* which made her beatification possible in 1980, during John Paul II's immense enthusiasm about indigenous peoples at a time when inculturation was very much in vogue (inculturation especially in the sense of evangelization, including local customs, and no longer imposing a Western model, on the ground that Christ's message rises above all cultures).[2]

Kateri's cause would certainly not have succeeded without the intense campaign organized by thousands of Native American Catholics in the network of the Tekakwitha Conference.[3] Initially, this involved an annual conference of a few missionaries trying to stem the desertions from tribal parishes. The first was held in 1939 at Fargo, ND. The timid reforms which they introduced increased when the time came to apply the decisions of Vatican II. In 1979, the assembly became the 'Tekakwitha Conference National Centre', based at Great Falls, MO. Since 1998, it has been run by the Director, Sister Kateri Mitchell, a binational Mohawk nun from the St Regis (Akwesasne) Reservation that straddles Northern Franklin County and Western Quebec. The average number of participants in the annual conference is about 800 to 1000. In 2008 the Conference took place at Edmonton, which shows the growing inclusion of Canadians. The aim of the Conference is to promote the physical, psychological and spiritual healing of Native peoples. The main unifying activity has been the campaign for Kateri's canonization.

In spite of this unanimity, it is important not to overlook the antagonism aroused by the Catholicized figure of Tekakwitha. Some Native Traditionalists who had jettisoned Catholicism and Christianity in general, and knew Kateri's story, condemned the hijacking of her Iroquois identity for colonialist ends. They argued, for instance, that her self-inflicted mortifications, promoted by the Jesuits as suffering in imitation of Jesus Christ, were no more than Iroquois mourning rites (cutting her hair, slashing her legs, putting glowing coals between her toes, and so on). She was said to have been all but forcibly confined in the mission. The historian Allan Greer has stressed Kateri's essentially 'Indian' character, and claims that she would not have had the strictly Catholic mystical experience described by the Jesuits, which they rehandled to show the effectiveness of their evangelization. According to Greer, she exhibited an amalgam of Iroquois religion and imported Catholicism.[4]

III Examination of the cause

Of course, when a cause is examined it has to suffer a relentless scrutiny of the supporters' motives. The animadversio transcribed in the positio on Kateri's virtues asked if the Jesuits had been tempted to embellish her qualities? Were their statements credible? The eventual response was categorical: the Jesuits could not lie, for if they did so they would be guilty of a grave sin. Moreover, if they had really wanted to show how successful their evangelization was, they would not have been content to advance the cause of only one individual, but would have embroidered the lives of several people. Yet the 'Jesuit Relations' (the voluminous annual documents sent by seventeenth-century Canadian Jesuits to their Paris office) contain no more than summary accounts of other virtuous Indians, with no explicit highlighting of their exemplary nature.

We should also consider those of Kateri's exemplary qualities that fit the typology of heroic virtues but are no longer especially valued by her followers. For example, in addition to the theological virtues of faith, hope and charity, hagiographers lay most emphasis on her virginity and repeated refusal to accept a husband, which would demonstrate her commitment to the Jesuits' and nuns' ideal way of life. In general, however, Native Americans and Canadians consider celibacy and virginity to be unnatural. They also constitute the main reason for a lack of vocations for the priesthood.

Indigenous Catholics do not call Kateri's virtues in question but pay them scant attention. We live in a different age, with different notions of heroic virtue. Admittedly, they see her as someone who dedicated her life to the Lord, but think of her even more as someone who devoted herself to her family and people in a time of military conquests that disrupted the equilibrium of her culture for ever. From now on, her virtues are an example for indigenous peoples bruised by centuries of conquest and deportation, and devastated by alcohol, drugs, unemployment, and family collapse. Kateri lived in an age of transition and is seen as a model of physical and moral survival. The theme of the 73rd Annual Tekakwitha Conference in Albany (July 2012), near her American shrine, was 'Walking in her footsteps in Kateri country'. Her merits are vaunted as those of a strong woman and pioneer feminist. Since she liked to pray in the woods, she has been declared 'patron of the environment and ecology' along with St Francis of Assisi. Her feast day is 14 July. An increasing number of parishes in North America have put themselves under her protection over the last 20 years.

The decree for her canonization was thought to be timely. The enthusiasm for Kateri was not fading, but disillusionment with the institutional Church was increasing proportionately. Native American

Catholics are very respectful towards their local clergy, but lack confidence in the hierarchy. Many of them thought that the bishops were not doing enough to accelerate the canonization. They suspected the existence of various other motives for the delay, such as Rome's inability to decide which country she should be assigned to as a saint, for she was born in one and died in another. This interpretation was advanced mainly by Michael Stogre SJ (Director of the Anishinabe Spiritual Centre in Espanola, Ontario, from 2006 to 2010). Rome was also said to have extended the delay because, once the objective was achieved, the Kateri campaign would vanish along with its justification.[5]

IV A miracle of the first class

In fact, to progress further, Kateri's cause required a 'miracle of the first class'. In 2006 one duly occurred near Seattle. A little boy, Jake Finkbonner, cut his lip while playing basket-ball. He developed a fulminating septicaemia, a fatal 'flesh-eating' infection. The parents were told that he could not be saved. They had heard of Blessed Kateri because the father was part Lummi (an indigenous American nation whose members now live in Washington State). Their parish priest asked the congregation to pray to Tekakwitha and the prayer effort spread. Sister Kateri Mitchell brought along a relic of Tekakwitha when asked to do so. The relic was brought into contact with the child. A few hours later, to the doctors' amazement, the infection began to recede. I saw the inexplicably-cured child, his still ravaged face partially covered by a plastic mask, when his family brought him to the Tekakwitha Conference at Burien/Seattle (July 2006). Five years of investigations by the group of doctors reporting to the Sacred Congregation for the Causes of Saints were needed to establish that, in the current state of knowledge, there was no medical explanation for this cure. The theologians concluded that the child had been healed through the intercession of the Blessed Kateri.

On 21 October 2012, Pope Benedict XVI received the indigenous North American Catholics in St Peter's. From now on they will be fully recognized by the body to which to which they have remained faithful for centuries against all odds. Now that Kateri has been canonized, their campaign to improve the material and spiritual life of their people will gain in strength and confidence.[6]

Translated by Felicity Leng

Notes

1. Bernadette Rigal-Cellard, 'La Vierge est une Amérindienne: Kateri Tekakwitha, à l'extrême imitation de Jésus et de Marie', in B. Rigal-Cellard (ed), *Missions extrêmes: en Amérique du Nord: des Jésuites à Raël*, Bordeaux, 2005, pp. 124–56.
2. Cf. in this regard Achiel Peelman, OMI, *Le Christ est amérindien: une réflexion théologique sur l'inculturation du Christ parmi les Amérindiens du Canada*, Outremont, Quebec, 1992 (ET: *Christ is a Native American*, Ottawa & Maryknoll, NY, 1995).
3. Paula Elizabeth Holmes, '"We are Native Catholics": Inculturation and the Tekakwitha Conference', *Studies in Religion/Sciences Religieuses* 28.2 (1999), pp. 153–74; *id.*, *Symbol Tales: Paths Towards the Creation of a Saint* [doctoral thesis], Hamilton, Ontario, 2000.
4. Allan Greer, *Mohawk Saint: Catherine Tekakwitha and the Jesuits*, New York, 2005; *id.*, & Jodi Bilinkoff (eds), *Colonial Saints: Discovering the Holy in the Americas*, New York, 2003; Joëlle Rostkowski, *La conversion inachevée: les Indiens et le christianisme*, Paris, 1998.
5. Cf. Christopher Vecsey, *The Paths of Kateri's Kin*, Notre Dame, Indiana, 1997, p. 103; Michael Stogre, SJ, *Pensée sociale chrétienne et droits des Aborigènes*, Montreal, 1993.
6. For further reading, see Marie Thérèse Archambault, Christopher Vecsey & Mark G. Thiel (eds), *The Crossing of Two Roads: Being Catholic and Native in the United States*, Maryknoll, NY, 2003.

Women as Pioneers at Vatican II

IDA RAMING

I Introduction

As an event of vast scope concerned with church policy, even after 50 years the Second Vatican Council still exerts a determinative influence on theological discourse within and outside the Roman Catholic Church.[1] Nevertheless, due consideration is scarcely ever given to the fact that 50 per cent of the 'people of God' (Dogmatic Constitution on the Church, *Lumen gentium* 9), which means women, weren't even present at the Council initially. It was only from the third session (September 1964) that a small group of carefully-selected women were allowed entry as so-called 'auditors' (without any voting rights, of course). In a gripping book with the significant title *Guests in Their Own House*,[2] Carmel McEnroy describes the impressions and testimonies of this tiny group of auditors. She tells of the very considerable misogyny of many conciliar 'Fathers' at the beginning, and how, with the aid of a few courageous theologians (such as Bernard Häring) and bishops (Suenens, Malula, Coderre), they were able to exert a definite though very limited influence on a few formulations in the conciliar documents, in the last two phases of the Council.

Through the no more than 'symbolic' presence of a few women, an 'outside' initiative was able to affect this 'closed' male conciliar society. A number of legally and theologically trained women, who had observed the preparations for the Council attentively, confronted this entirely male church assembly with their call for women to be ranked and valued in accordance with the times we live in.

II The first petition to the Council for the ordination of women

In the then widespread atmosphere of disregard for women, and the notion of their second-class status and inferiority, the Swiss lawyer Gertrud Heinzelmann (1914–99), holder of a doctorate in law, first raised the demand for women's ordination publicly and emphatically. In May 1962, even before the Council began, she sent a comprehensive submission to the preparatory Commission, which she introduced with these rousing words: 'I address you as a woman of our own times who is well aware of her sisters' needs and problems as a result of her studies, profession and many years of activity in the women's movement. I turn to you hoping that my petition will receive the attention which it deserves in view of the seriousness and weight of the subject-matter.... I trust that what I say will be taken as intended: as the grievance and appeal of half the human race; of female humankind, oppressed for thousands of years and suffering a repression to which the Church with its theory about women has contributed and still contributes in a way deeply harmful to the Christian conscience and awareness.'[3] As a Catholic woman and lawyer who had already campaigned for many years for political voting rights for women in Switzerland, she was conscious of the fateful influence of misogynistic church attitudes on society in general. While working on her thesis on constitutional law and church–state relations, she came upon pronouncements by Fathers and Doctors of the Church that could only be termed discriminatory as far as women were concerned. She had also prepared an extensive collection of texts from the works of Thomas Aquinas with her own critical commentaries, to which she referred when preparing her contribution to the Council. Her submission includes a critical rejection of the ontic depreciation of women (under the influence of Aristotelian ideas) in the works of Aquinas[4], whom the official Church credited with a special authority as a Doctor of the Church. Heinzelmann derived the possibility in principle and requirement of women's ordination from the favourable pronouncements of Aquinas on the spiritual nature of humans and on the sacraments in general. In this she was guided by the hope that: 'if the official Church were now to discard formally the ballast of medieval natural doctrine on women, the way to women becoming priests would be open on the basis of purified Thomist teaching, of the actual *philosophia rationalis* with regard to humanity'.[5] The publication of her petition to the Council assured her that 'she had achieved a leap forward for the spiritual progress of women that could never be revised. Even a later Council would have to recall that already, at Vatican II, full equality in the Church and the ordained ministry for women had been shown to be requisite'.[6]

III Further submissions to the Council: the debate becomes more intense....

As might be expected, Heinzelmann's petition elicited strong reactions for and against. Some Swiss newspapers made offensive attacks on the author and poured scorn and derision on her. On the other hand, positive reactions showed that 'many people had been thinking along the same lines ... at the same time'.[7] This was the source of the first contacts with German women theologians. In 1959 one of them, Josefa Theresia Münch, a qualified theologian, had already sent the Vatican several (unpublished) requests for changes in canon law (c. 968 §1 CIC/1917) that excluded women from sacramental ordination. At the first German-language press conference (October 1962), she posed the well-grounded question whether women too should not be invited to attend the Council. The reaction to this question was a mixture of embarrassment, indignation and laughter. Finally the director of the German press centre, Bishop Kampe, half-reassuringly and half in jest, replied that women too would be able to attend 'Vatican III!'.[8]

IV A petition to the Council by Iris Müller and Ida Raming (1963)

When they were students in the Catholic theology faculty of the University of Münster in the early 1960s, first Iris Müller (1930–2011), and a little later she and Ida Raming (author of this article), had critically examined the grounds for excluding women from ordination and the priesthood. They were able to revert to this reasoned preparatory work when they composed their own submission to the Council in 1963.

In theological discourse at that time, the following arguments were advanced for barring women from ordination and the priesthood: 1. Women were subordinate to men in the order of creation; 2. Women's nature prevents them from exercising a priestly ministry; 3. Christ entered the world as a man; 4. Christ chose only men as apostles; 5. The apostle Paul's pronouncements on the position of women, especially his instructions on their behaviour during divine service (cf. 1 Cor. 11.2–16; 1 Cor. 14.34; 1 Tim. 2.11–15), and his interpretation of woman as the image of the Church (Eph. 5.22ff), are irreconcilable with the transmission of the priesthood to women; 6. Even Mary herself as the Mother of God did not receive the priesthood; 7.The polarity of the sexes would have a disturbing effect in the sanctuary; 8. To date the Church has kept unequivocally to its traditional views in this respect.

In their submission, Iris Müller and Ida Raming attempted to refute all these arguments with reference to the theological–critical state of knowledge at that time.[9]

It is remarkable that nowadays the church leadership should still cite most of these arguments, especially those derived from the New Testament, as evidence against the admission of women to the priesthood, even though, according to the report of the Papal Bible Commission of 1976, the New Testament yields no sustainable arguments for excluding women from the priestly ministry. Nevertheless, in its *Declaration on the Question of the Admission of Women to the Ministerial Priesthood* (*Inter insigniores*; 1976, published 1977), the Sacred Congregation for the Doctrine of the Faith disregarded this research finding. A serious deadlock is apparent in the thinking and judgement of the Vatican church leadership, which still ignores the results of exegetical, dogmatic and historical research that have been available for a long time.

For instance, the declaration *Inter insigniores* still stresses the following: '...when Christ's role in the Eucharist is to be expressed sacramentally, there would not be this 'natural resemblance' which must exist between Christ and his minister if the role of Christ were not taken by a man: in such a case it would be difficult to see in the minister the image of Christ. For Christ himself was and remains a man...'.[10] The two women theologians had already argued against this notion in their submission: '...Against the conservative conception that derives the consequence of the exclusion of women from the priesthood from the assumption of male gender by the Logos, thereby attributing a special significance to his gender, it is to be asserted decisively that fundamental significance is to be assigned *only to the fact that Christ (or the Logos) became human*; the aspect of gender is wholly irrelevant here; for it is not Christ 'becoming a man' that has a redemptive function, but solely his becoming a human being, in accordance with the evidence of Scripture in Jn. 1.14; Phil. 2.6ff, and so on....'.[11]

Heinzelmann's contribution to the Council reached Iris Müller and Ida Raming in a roundabout way. They were overjoyed that a Catholic woman from Switzerland was responsible for this courageous initiative. In 1963 a personal meeting took place in Münster between the women theologians J. T. Münch, I. Müller, I. Raming and Gertrud Heinzelmann. In 1963 news of the submission also brought an announcement from the USA by Dr Rosemary Lauer, who taught at St John's University (New York). She published several articles on the theme of 'Women and the Church' in the journal *Commonweal*. She also commissioned an English translation of Heinzelmann's submission for the American press. These publications alerted Mary Daly for the first time to the existence of Heinzelmann's submission. In the 1960s Daly studied theology at the University of Fribourg, and in 1964 became the first woman and American to be awarded a doctorate in theology there.

V Collected petitions to the Council...

Contacts with the abovementioned six women led to the German–English book edited by Heinzelmann: *Wir schweigen nicht länger! Frauen äussern sich zum II. Vatikanischen Konzil* (1964). In addition to Heinzelmann's petition, it contains the conciliar submissions of Münch and that of Müller and Raming, as well as articles by Lauer and Daly from the time of the Council. For the first time, the book offers a systematic critical analysis of the various biblical and dogmatic grounds for excluding women from the priesthood. This analysis is the basis of a demand for full equality of rights in the ministry of the Roman Catholic Church. The book also insists on a reform of male-biased liturgical language (J. T. Münch's contribution). This publication gave considerable impetus to discussion of women's ordination and their admission to the priestly ministry, and influenced conciliar proceedings, though at a later point.

VI Pacem in terris: human rights for women

With his 1963 encyclical *Pacem in terris* (1963), John XXIII, the Vatican II pope, gave a firm impetus to the women's movement, which was at an early stage of development in the Church at the time. For the first time a papal encyclical treated women as subjects and bearers of human rights, for John XXIII assessed the movement for women's emancipation as a 'sign of the times that demanded consideration': 'Women, who are now increasingly conscious of their human dignity, are very far from allowing themselves to be treated as some soulless material or as mere instruments; instead they seek to ensure that they are accorded rights and duties, in domestic life as in the State, that are appropriate to the dignity of the human person ...' (22). Human beings 'also have the inalienable right to give the societies of which they are members the form they consider most suitable for the aim they have in view, and to act within such societies and on their own initiative and on their own responsibility in order to achieve their desired objectives' (9). '...if humans become conscious of their rights, they must become equally aware of their duties. Thus those who possess certain rights have likewise the duty to claim those rights as marks of their dignity, while all others have the obligation to acknowledge those rights and respect them...' (24).

These were encouraging words, but also an urgent warning that could not be passed over entirely, even in the conciliar assembly. The programmatic declaration from the Pastoral Constitution on the Church in the modern world, *Gaudium et spes* (29), seems to echo the words of the encyclical: 'All humans are endowed with a rational soul and are created in God's image; they have the same nature and origin and, being redeemed by Christ, they enjoy the same divine calling and destiny; there is here a basic equality between all humans and it must be given ever greater recognition...forms of social or cultural discrimination in basic personal rights on the grounds of sex, race, colour, social conditions, language or religion, must be curbed and eradicated as incompatible with God's design.'

Although this programmatic pronouncement contains several important points of reference as well as prerequisites for overcoming the severe discrimination against women within the Church (in particular their exclusion from all offices of the ordained priesthood merely because they are women), no reforms in this regard are deduced from those indications and conditions, or even contemplated in any way whatsoever.

VII Positive effects of 'We won't keep silence any longer...'

The topic of women's ordination was not heard directly but was in fact taboo at the Council assembly itself. Even the few women auditors present did not voice it or advocate it.

This theme was raised expressly in only one intervention at the Council (October 1965), by Archbishop Paul Hallinan (Atlanta, USA).

He not only requested that women should undertake the offices of readers and acolytes during divine service, but that women should be admitted to the office of deacon; and suggested furthermore that women should take part in theological instruction and in the revision of the *Codex iuris canonici* (Code of Canon Law). His courageous proposal could be attributed to the direct influence of the journalist and peritus (for the American bishops) Placidus Jordan OSB, who had disseminated the collected conciliar petitions in the American bishops' conference and outside.[12] But this was shortly before the end of the Council, so that the Archbishop's intervention was not reflected in the conciliar documents.

VIII   Reactions to 'We won't keep silence any longer...!'

'Women and the Church' certainly became a more vital topic outside the actual Council in its final phase. Several articles supporting this feminist initiative appeared in response to the book. But traditionalist circles in the Vatican attempted a counter-attack. Immediately before the end of the Council (November 1965), with express reference to 'We won't keep silence any longer...!', though significantly without any more detailed bibliography, the *Osservatore Romano* published an entire series of articles on *La donna e il Sacerdozio* (Women and the Priesthood) by the traditionalist Franciscan priest Gino Concetti. He wrote in his introduction: 'The atmosphere of zealous initiatives which preceded and accompanied Vatican II led to many others, including one that attempts to draw the attention of the responsible hierarchy to the extension of the ministerial priesthood to women...'[13]

His final conclusion, based on traditional texts discriminating against women, is as follows: 'If he had wanted to, Christ would have singled out women...for elevation to the priesthood. He did not elevate them thus, not in order to accord with a human tradition of the world around him at the time, but out of respect for the order of creation and God's plan of salvation, both of which call for male dominance: the supremacy of the old Adam and the new Christ...'.[14]

The entire article is so to speak a harbinger of later pronouncements of the Vatican church leadership directed against the notion of women priests (*Inter Insigniores*, 1977; *Ordinatio Sacerdotalis*, 1994). Both before and during the Council, those pioneer women, and later many other major theologians, men and women, have offered reasoned objections to these ideas. It is scandalous that the positive consequences of these analyses, insights and claims are still outstanding.

Translated by J. G. Cumming

Notes

1. The article is based on: Ida Raming, 'Frauen stehen auf gegen Diskriminierung und Entrechtung des weiblichen Geschlechts in der Kirche', in: Iris Müller & Ida Raming, *Unser Leben im Einsatz für Menschenrechte der Frauen in der römisch-katholischen Kirche*, Münster, 2007, pp. 220–48.
2. *The Women of Vatican II*, New York, 1996.
3. G. Heinzelmann, *Wir schweigen nicht länger! We Won't Keep Silence Any Longer! Frauen äussern sich zum II. Vatikanischen Konzil*, Zürich, 1964, p. 20.
4. 'Women are subject to men on account of their inherent natural weakness and because of the strength of the male intellect and physique .... Man is the principle for woman and her objective just as God is the principle for the creature as a whole and its objective...' G. Heinzelmann, *op. cit. supra*, pp. 25–6.
5. G. Heinzelmann, *Die geheiligte Diskriminierung. Beiträge zum kirchlichen Feminismus*, Bonstetten, 1986, p. 97.
6. *Ibid.*, p. 112.
7. *Ibid.*, p. 90.
8. *Ibid.*, p. 121.
9. Cf. G. Heinzelmann, 'Wir schweigen...', *op. cit.*, pp. 61–76 and I. Müller & G. Raming, *Unser Leben im Einsatz...* , *op. cit.*, , pp.136–54.
10. *Inter Insigniores*, No. 5.
11. G. Heinzelmann 'Wir schweigen...', *op. cit.*, p. 66; cf. I. Müller & G. Raming, *Unser Leben im Einsatz...*, *op. cit.*, p. 142.
12. Cf. G. Heinzelmann, *Die geheiligte Diskriminierung...*, *op. cit.*, p. 138.
13. G. Heinzelmann, *Die getrennten Schwestern. Frauen nach dem Konzil*, Zürich, 1967, p. 99.
14. *Ibid.*

Contributors

MARK J. ALLMAN is Professor of Religious & Theological Studies at Merrimack College, MA, USA. His publications include: 'Theology H2O: The World Water Crisis and Sacramental Imagination', in *Green Discipleship: Catholic Theological Ethics and the Environment* (2011); *The Almighty and the Dollar: Reflections on Economic Justice for All* (2012); *After the Smoke Clears: The Just War Tradition and Post War Justice* (with Tobias Winright, 2010); and *Who Would Jesus Kill? War, Peace and the Christian Tradition* (2008), which won the College Theology Society Book of the Year Award.

Address: Department of Religious & Theological Studies, Merrimack College, 315 Turnpike Street, North Andover, MA 01845, USA.
Email: allmanm@merrimack.edu

MARCELO BARROS OSB is a Brazilian Benedictine monk, theologian and author. He is presently Latin-American co-ordinator of the Ecumenical Association of Third-World Theologians (ASETT). He has published 44 books, including *O Espírito vem pelas Águas*, 2003.

Address: Rua Arnoldo Magalhães, 243, apartamento 02, Casa Amarela, 52051- 280 Recife – PE, Brazil.
Email: irmarcelobarros@uol.com.br

ANNE-BEATRICE FAYE CIC is a Sengalese nun of the Order of the Sisters of Our Lady of the Immaculate Conception of Castres. She received her doctorate in philosophy from the Cheik Anta Diop University in Dakar, Senegal. One of her special interests is the promotion of women in the African context. She is currently Professor of Philosophy and a member of the Association of African Theologians

(ATA). She has been a member of the General Council of her Institute in Rome since 2008.

Address: Via Vincenzo Viara de Ricci, 24, 00168 – Rome – Italy.
Email: cicbeafaye@yahoo.fr

ERHARD S. GERSTENBERGER was born in Rheinhausen, Germany, and studied Evangelical theology (1952–7). He spent five years in New Haven, Connecticut (Yale Divinity School). He was awarded a doctorate in OT studies at Bonn University with a thesis on *Wesen und Herkunft des 'apodiktischen' Rechts*, 1965, 22009). He was pastor of the parish of Essen-Frohnhausen (1965–75). He took his university teaching degree in Heidelberg (*Der bittende Mensch*, 1980). He was Reader in OT studies in São Leopoldo, RS, Brazil (1975–81) and Professor in Giessen and Marburg (1981–97). Recent publications include *Theologien im AT*, 2001; *Israel in der Perserzeit*, 2005; *Gesammelte Aufsätze 2012*: http://geb.uni-giessen.de/geb/volltexte/2012/8601/ = open access.

Address: Fasanenweg 29, 35394 Giessen, Germany
Email: gersterh@staff.uni-marburg.de

MARY E. HUNT is a feminist Catholic theologian and co-director of the Women's Alliance for Theology, Ethics and Ritual (WATER) in Silver Spring, MD, USA. Dr Hunt lectures and writes on theology and ethics. She is the editor of *A Guide for Women in Religion: Making Your Way from A to Z* (2004) and co-editor with Diann L. Neu of *New Feminist Christianity: Many Voices, Many Views* (2010).

Address: Women's Alliance for Theology, Ethics and Ritual (WATER), 8121 Georgia Ave. #310, Silver Spring, MD, 20910, USA.
Email: mhunt@hers.com

LUIS INFANTI OSM is a member of the Servants of Mary. He was born in Italy, and studied and was ordained as a priest in Bolivia. In 1999 he was consecrated Bishop of a poor region of the country with vast reserves of water, the Apostolic Vicariate of Aysén. Bishop Infanti took part in the socio-ecological movement of 2011–12, which earned him harsh criticism and condemnation by governmental authorities. His pastoral letter 'Danos hoy el agua de cada día' (1 September 2008) is evidence of an active presence of the Apostolic Vicariate in civic protest movements. See this document at www.iglesiadeaysen.cl/archivos/cartapastoral and a collection of his writings in *Huellas de una Iglesia profética en la Patagonia* (2011).

Address: Casilla 14-D, Coyhaique, Aysen, Chile.
Email: linfanti@episcopado.cl

ŽELJKO IVANKOVIĆ was born in Vareš in 1954. He is a writer and has produced thirty books of poetry, novels, essays, radio dramas and journalism. The verse collections include: *Le temps sans les verbes* (1986); *L'effondrement de l'image* (1990); *La recherche du pays natal* (1997); *La richesse, le clair de lune froid* (2002); *Jésus a lu le journal* (2006); *Le journal de la mélancolie* (2008); prose works include: *Les contes sur l'amour et la mort* (1989); *700 jours de siège* (1995); *Qui a allumé l'obscurité ?* (1995); *Les nouveaux contes sur l'amour et la mort* (2001); *Les contes de Vareš* (2003); *Sur son héritage*, (2010). Among his novels see: *Le monde commença aussi par le toucher* (1992); *L'amour à Berlin* (1995); for essays consult: *Les horizons I-III (1987–2000); En marges du chaos* (2001), *Le tatouage de l'identité* (2007), *Lire Ivanković à Sarajevo* (2010), *Un regard depuis les marges* (2011). He has received several prizes.

Address: Višnjik 44, BiH – 71000 Sarajevo, Bosnia-Herzogovina.
Email: zeljkoivankovic@yahoo.de

KUMIKO KATO was born into a Catholic family in Tokyo (Japan). He studied religion and exegesis at the University of Tokyo from 1984 to 1992. He studied in Paderborn (Germany) from 1992 to 1996. Since 1996 he has taught at various universities in Tokyo and his main research interest has been Hebrew Wisdom literature. His wife is a Japanese scholar of German language and literature and they have two children.

Address: Institute for Research on Christian Culture, University of the Sacred Heart, Tokyo, 4-3-1 Hiroo Shibuya-ku, Tokyo, 150-8938, Japan.
Email: nii93@za.cyberhome.ne.jp

KUNTALA LAHIRI-DUTT is a Fellow in the Resource Management in Asia Pacific Programme at the Australian National University in Canberra. Her publications on water include: *Fluid Bonds: Views on Gender and Water* (2006), and *Water First: Issues and Challenges for Nations and Communities in South Asia* (edited with Robert Wasson, 2008). Her forthcoming book *Dancing with the River: People and Lives on the Chars of South Asia* (April 2013) was written jointly with Gopa Samanta.

Address: College of Asia and the Pacific, Fellows Road, ACTON, ACT 0200,
Australia.
Email: Kuntala.Lahiri-Dutt@anu.edu.au

PIERRE LETOURNEAU is Professor of New Testament studies at the Faculty of Theology and Religious Studies of the University of Montreal. Among his recent publications are: *Le grec du Nouveau Testament: de l'alphabet aux phrases complexes* (2010); 'The *Dialog of the Savior* as a Witness of the Late Valentinian Tradition', in: *Vigiliae Christianae* (2010); 'Creation in Gnostic Christian Texts', in Tobias Nicklas & Korinna Zamfir (eds), *Creation in Early Jewish and Christian Literature* (2010); *Et vous, qui dites-vous que je suis? La gestion des personnages dans les récits bibliques* (co-edited with Michel Talbot, 2007).

Address: Faculty of Theology and Science of Religions, Montreal University, C.P. 6128, succ. Centre-ville, Montréal, Quebec, H3C 3J7, Canada.
Email: pierre.letourneau@umontreal.ca

Contributors

LENA PARTZSCH studied at the Political Studies Institute in Strasbourg and the Free University of Berlin, and was awarded degrees there in 2003 and 2007. She worked simultaneously as a scientific researcher in the European Parliament and German Parliament. She is Deputy Director of the socio-ecological research group GETIDOS (Getting Things Done Sustainably) at the University of Greifswald, Germany. Since 2009, her research project leading to a university teaching degree has concerned the part played in international relations by private individuals such as philanthropists, celebrities and social entrepreneurs. She directed an interdisciplinary water project at the Helmholtz Centre for Environmental Research (2007–9) and was a member of the 'Ökologie und Fairness im Welthandelsregime' group at the Heinrich-Böll Foundation and Wuppertal Institute (2004–7).

Address: GETIDOS Socio-ecological Research Group, University of Greifswald, Soldmannstrasse 23, 17489 Greifswald, Germany.
Email: lena.partzsch@uni-greifswald.de

IDA RAMING studied philosophy, theology and German language and literature in Münster and Freiburg. Her doctoral dissertation discussed the exclusion of women from the priesthood. She was a research assistant at Münster University, taught in schools, and became an adviser to *Concilium* on feminist theology. Her publications include: *Frauenbewegung und Kirche* (1989, ²1991); *Frauen finden einen Weg: Die internationale Bewegung Römisch-Katholische Priesterinnen*, with co-editors (2009). After more than 40 years of argument in favour of women's ordination, she was ordained an RC priest 'contra legem' in June 2002, as a prophetic sign against the oppression of women.

Address: Im Asemwald 32/10, 70599 Stuttgart, Germany.
Email: iraming@t-online.de

BERNADETTE RIGAL-CELLARD holds a French higher teaching degree in English. She is Professor in North-American studies at Bordeaux University 3, and teaches a course on religion and societies and in the Canadian Studies Centre. She specializes in North American minority religions and indigenous literature. Her publications include: *Le Mythe et la plume: La littérature des Indiens d'Amérique du Nord* (2004); *La religion des Mormons* (2012); *Missions Extrêmes en Amérique du Nord: des jésuites à Raël* (2005); *Religions et mondialisation: exils, expansions, résistances* (2009); *Prophéties et utopies religieuses au Canada* (2011).

Address: 29 rue Brachet, 33200 Bordeaux, France.
E-mail: bcellard@numericable.fr

SYLVIE SHAW lectures on studies in religion at the University of Queensland, Australia. Her research interests are at the intersection of religion and ecology. She is involved in a study which traverses the waterways of South-East Queensland, focusing on people's valuations of terrestrial and marine waterways. Her publications include *Deep Blue: Critical Reflections on Nature Religion and Water* (2008, with Andrew Francis); and a major study on the impact of fisheries change in Queensland: *Identifying, Communicating and Integrating Social Considerations into Future Management Concerns in Inshore Commercial Fisheries in Coastal Queensland* (2011, with Helen Johnson & Wolfram Dressler).

Address: School of HPRC, The University of Queensland, St Lucia, 4067, Queensland, Australia.
Email: sylvie.shaw@uq.edu.au

CONCILIUM
International Journal of Theology

FOUNDERS
Anton van den Boogaard; Paul Brand; Yves Congar, OP; Hans Küng;
Johann Baptist Metz; Karl Rahner, SJ; Edward Schillebeeckx

BOARD OF DIRECTORS
President: Felix Wilfred
Vice Presidents: Erik Borgman; Diego Irarrázaval; Susan Ross

BOARD OF EDITORS
Regina Ammicht Quinn (Frankfurt, Germany)
Mike Babić
Maria Clara Bingemer (Rio de Janeiro, Brazil)
Erik Borgman (Nijmegen, The Netherlands)
Lisa Sowle Cahill (Boston, USA)
Frère Thierry Marie Courau (France)
Hille Haker (Frankfurt, Germany)
Diego Irarrázaval (Santiago, Chile)
Solange Lefebvre (Montreal, Canada)
Eloi Messi Metogo (Yaounde, Cameroon)
Sarojini Nadar (Durban, South Africa)
Daniel Franklin Pilario (Quezon City, Philippines)
Susan Ross (Chicago, USA)
Silvia Scatena (Reggio Emilia, Italy)
Jon Sobrino SJ (San Salvador, El Salvador)
Luiz Carlos Susin (Porto Alegre, Brazil)
Andres Torres Queiruga (Santiago de Compostela, Spain)
João J. Viba-Chã (Portugal)
Marie-Theres Wacker (Münster, Germany)
Felix Wilfred (Madras, India)

PUBLISHERS
SCM Press (London, UK)
Matthias-Grünewald Verlag (Ostfildern, Germany)
Editrice Queriniana (Brescia, Italy)
Editorial Verbo Divino (Estella, Spain)
EditoraVozes (Petropolis, Brazil)
Ex Libris and Synopsis (Rijeka, Croatia)

Concilium Secretariat:
Asian Centre for Cross-Cultural Studies,
40/6A, Panayur Kuppam Road, Sholinganallur Post, Panayur, Madras 600119, India.
Phone: +91- 44 24530682 Fax: +91- 44 24530443
E-mail: Concilium.madras@gmail.com
Managing Secretary: Arokia Mary Anthonidas

Concilium Subscription Information

February	**2013/1:**	*Reconciliation: Empowering Grace*
April	**2013/2:**	*Postcolonial Theology*
August	**2013/3:**	*Saints and Sanctity Today*
October	**2013/4:**	*The Ambivalence of Sacrifice*
December	**2013/5:**	*Orthodoxy*

New subscribers: to receive *Concilium 2013* (five issues) anywhere in the world, please copy this form, complete it in block capitals and send it with your payment to the address below.

Please enter my subscription for *Concilium 2013*

Individuals
____ £50 UK
____ £72 overseas and Eire
____ $95 North America/Rest of World
____ €85 Europe

Institutions
____ £72 UK
____ £92 overseas and Eire
____ $110 North America/Rest of World
____ €135 Europe

Postage included – airmail for overseas subscribers

Payment Details:
Payment must accompany all orders and can be made by cheque or credit card
I enclose a cheque for £/$/€ _____ Payable to Hymns Ancient and Modern Ltd
Please charge my Visa/MasterCard (Delete as appropriate) for £/$/€ _____

Credit card number _____

Expiry date _____

Signature of cardholder_____

Name on card _____

Telephone _____ E-mail _____

Send your order to *Concilium,* **Hymns Ancient and Modern Ltd**
13a Hellesdon Park Road, Norwich NR6 5DR, UK
E-mail: concilium@hymnsam.co.uk
or order online at www.conciliumjournal.co.uk

Customer service information
All orders must be prepaid. Subscriptions are entered on an annual basis (i.e. January to December). No refunds on subscriptions will be made after the first issue of the Journal has been despatched. If you have any queries or require Information about other payment methods, please contact our Customer Services department.

www.ingramcontent.com/pod-product-compliance
Lightning Source LLC
Chambersburg PA
CBHW051403290426
44108CB00015B/2138